EINSTEIN'S PUZZLE UNIVERSE

The publishers would like to thank the following sources for their kind permission to reproduce the pictures in this book.

Alamy, Bridgeman Images, Dover Books, Getty Images, NASA, National Portrait Gallery, London, Shutterstock.com & Thinkstock.com

THIS IS A CARLTON BOOK

This edition published in 2015
by Carlton Books Limited
20 Mortimer Street
London W1T 3JW

Art Direction: Stephen Cary
Editorial: Caroline Curtis
Puzzle Checker: Richard Cater
Designer: Drew McGovern
Project Editor: Matthew Lowing

ISBN 978-1-78097-633-4

10 9 8 7 6 5 4 3

Printed in China

$$E=mc^2$$

EINSTEIN'S PUZZLE UNIVERSE

**"Relatively" difficult riddles & conundrums
inspired by the great scientist**

Tim Dedopulos

CARLTON
BOOKS

CONTENTS

CHAPTER TWO

CHAPTER THREE

CHAPTER FOUR

CHAPTER FIVE

INTRODUCTION

Albert Einstein was the defining genius of the twentieth century. We remember him as a brilliant and dazzlingly inventive scientist, and as an eccentric dresser with a crazy head of hair. We tend to forget his other impacts – as the fierce opponent of racism who marched in favour of African American rights, as the devoted lover of peace who saved thousands from Nazi pogroms, as the gifted violinist, even as the influential celebrity who helped start the nuclear era.

When *Time* magazine selected Einstein as their Person of the Century in 1999, it was no more than an honest recognition of his impact on our world. In his lifetime, he revolutionized our understanding of the universe and made possible most of the technologies that modernity depends on.

All of which presents something of a problem for the author of this volume. In creating the puzzles for this book, I have tried to select problems that Einstein might have found of some value, or that may have reflected his interests and inclinations. At the same time, I have tried to avoid turning his life into some sort of mawkish puzzle slideshow, so I've avoided the temptation to try cramming puzzles into his biography.

I would never try to speak for the great man himself, but if this book makes you think even a little about the nature of the world and universe we live in, that's all that I could ask for. Well, that and your enjoyment, of course.

Tim Dedopulos
London, 2015

$$\frac{d\gamma}{d\beta} = \frac{d}{d\beta}\left(\frac{1}{(1-\beta^2)^{1/2}}\right) = -\frac{1}{2}(-2\beta)(1-\beta^2)^{-3/2} = \beta(1-\beta^2)^{-3/2} \quad \therefore \quad F = m_0\left[\gamma\frac{dv}{dt} + v\frac{d\gamma}{dt}\right]$$

CHAPTER ONE

"You see, wire telegraph is a kind of a very, very long cat. You pull his tail in New York and his head is meowing in Los Angeles. Do you understand this? And radio operates exactly the same way: you send signals here, they receive them there. The only difference is that there is no cat."

ALBERT EINSTEIN

1
BODIES IN MOTION

We are used to the idea that it is possible to sit still, and pass time in a motionless manner. But this amazing planet of ours is very far from static. At all times, we are hurtling through the gulfs of space at astonishing velocities.

It may seem to casual thought that from the Sun's viewpoint, all of Earth's population is moving at the same speed. After all, our planet revolves around it at a steady 30km per second – anticlockwise, if we are looking from above the North Pole. However, there is another factor to consider. The Earth spins on its axis as it rotates, at a speed of around 28km per minute, if you are at the equator.

You know, of course, that from the surface of the planet, the Sun appears to rise in the east. So, are you moving more swiftly during the day, or at night?

Solution on page 160

ABSOLUTELY NOTHING

It is tempting, soothing even, to think of mathematics as a perfect edifice of logic and order. The truth however is that it is an art as well as a science, and it has places where absolutism breaks down.

For this example, we will show that 0 = 1. Firstly, however, I should point out that when adding a series of numbers, the associative law says that you may bracket the sums as you like without any effect. 1+2+3 = 1+ (2+3) = (1+2) +3.

So, with that established, consider adding an infinite number of zeroes. No matter how much nothing you gather, you will still always have nothing.
0 = 0+0+0+0+0+...

Since 1-1 = 0, you can replace each zero in your sum, like so:
0 = (1-1)+(1-1)+(1-1)+(1-1)+(1-1)+...

From the associative law, you may rearrange the brackets in your sum as you see fit. Which means:
0 = 1+(-1+1) +(-1+1) +(-1+1) +(-1+1) +(-1+1)+...

However, as established, (-1+1) = 0, so this sequence can also be stated as:
0 = 1 +0+0+0+0+0+...

Or, for simplicity's sake:

$$0 = 1.$$

Something is clearly incorrect. But what?

Solution on page 160

3
AN EXERCISE IN LOGIC

The English mathematician and author Lewis Carroll devised a series of excellent logical problems designed to illustrate and test deductive reasoning. Several statements are given below. You may assume – for the duration of this problem – that they are absolutely true in all particulars. From that assumption, you should be able to provide an answer to the question that follows.

I dislike things that cannot be put to use as a bridge.

Sunset clouds are unable to bear my weight.

The only subjects I enjoy poems about are things which I would welcome as a gift.

Anything which can be used as a bridge is able to bear my weight.

I would not accept a gift of a thing I disliked.

Would I enjoy a poem about sunset clouds?

Solution on page 161

4

SUBMERSIBLE

There are many pressing concerns when one is in a submarine, whether it is a time of war or not. However, one of the most important is for the captain to ensure that his boat not be permitted to rest on the bedrock of the ocean floor, even for a moment. Such an event may well prove fatal for the entire crew.

Can you say why?

Solution on page 161

> **Learn from yesterday, live for today, hope for tomorrow. The important thing is not to stop questioning.**
>
> **ALBERT EINSTEIN**

FORTY-EIGHT

Many numbers, particularly in the lower orders, can make a good claim for being of particular interest. It is in the realm of square numbers that 48 is of especial curiosity. If you add 1 to it, you get a square number [48+1 = 49 = 7x7], and if instead you halve it and add 1 to the result, you get a different square number [(48/2 = 24)+1 = 25 = 5x5]. Individually, the two conditions are trivially common, but taken together this way, they are less so.

In fact, 48 is the smallest number to satisfy both conditions. Can you find the next smallest to do so?

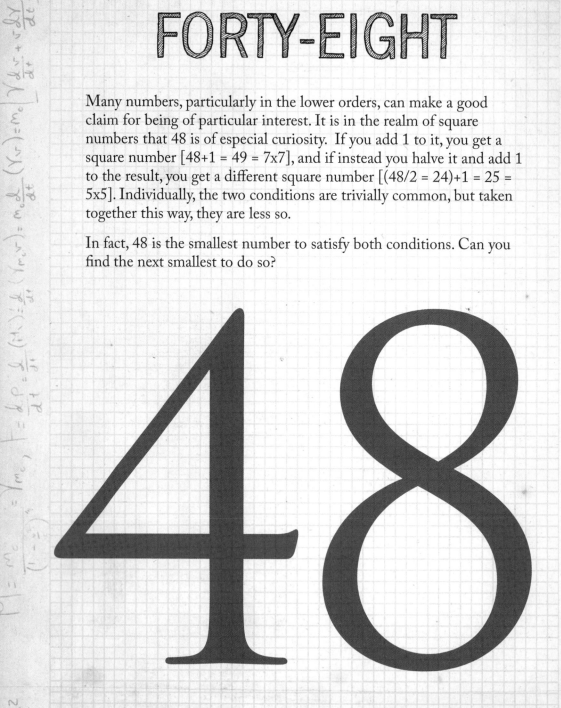

Solution on page 162

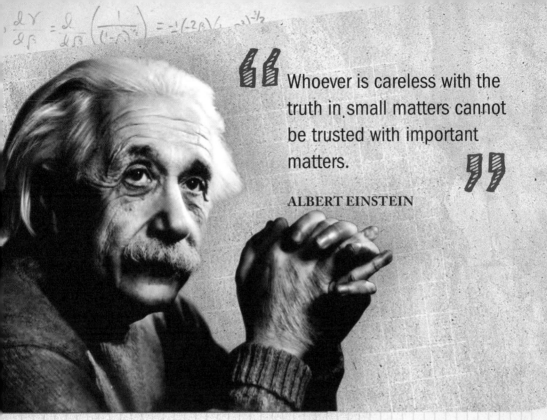

> Whoever is careless with the truth in small matters cannot be trusted with important matters.

ALBERT EINSTEIN

MASHED QUOTE

The puzzle below holds a well-known quotation. Although the words in each line remain in the correct order, all punctuation has been removed, and the lines themselves have been jumbled up.

Are you able to piece the original quotation back together?

LIKE AN HOUR THAT'S RELATIVITY
LIKE A SECOND WHEN
NICE GIRL AN HOUR SEEMS
HOT CINDER A SECOND SEEMS
WHEN YOU ARE COURTING A
YOU SIT ON A RED
ALBERT EINSTEIN

Solution on page 162

TWO PAILS

Imagine that you are in possession of two pails of water. These pails are identical in every significant respect, save that one has a large chunk of wood floating freely inside it, while the other does not. Apart from that disparity, the two are filled precisely to the brim with freshly distilled water.

Which of the pails would be the heavier?

Solution on page 163

8
HIGH WIRE

An incredible amount of skill, dedication and fitness is required to master the art of high-wire walking. However, when you see such a masterful athlete proceeding to and fro over a dizzying drop armed with nothing more than a long, saggy bar, bear in mind that perhaps the feat is somewhat less insanely risky than it may appear.

Can you say why?

Solution on page 163

9
CIPHERTEXT

In this puzzle, the challenge is to decrypt a quotation that has been made obscure by the use of a simple cipher. Are you able to work out what it says?

```
AHUMA NBEIN GISAP ARTOF THEWH OLECA LLEDB
YUSUN IVERS EAPAR TLIMI TEDIN TIMEA NDSPA
CEHEE XPERI ENCES HIMSE LFHIS THOUG HTSAN
DFEEL INGAS SOMET HINGS EPARA TEDFR OMTHE
RESTA KINDO FOPTI CALDE LUSIO NOFHI SCONS
CIOUS NESST HISDE LUSIO NISAK INDOF PRISO
NFORU SREST RICTI NGUST OOURP ERSON ALDES
IRESA NDTOA FFECT IONFO RAFEW PERSO NSNEA
RESTT OUSOU RTASK MUSTB ETOFR EEOUR SELVE
SFROM THISP RISON BYWID ENING OURCI RCLEO
FCOMP ASSIO NTOEM BRACE ALLLI VINGC REATU
RESAN DTHEW HOLEO FNATU REINI TSBEA UTYAL
BERTE INSTE INAHU
```

Solution on page 164

FIBONACCI'S GAME

This mathematical party game was devised in the thirteenth century by the Italian mathematician Leonardo Pisano, known to the modern world as Fibonacci. His work on the mathematical systems helped to set up the Renaissance, but the matter we will address here is less weighty.

Between two and nine people sit in a line, and together, they secretly conspire to select one of their number. This person picks a finger joint of one of their hands, either where a ring is being worn, or where the volunteer nominates as a spot where he or she would like to have a ring. The volunteer then takes their position in the line, doubles it, adds 5, multiplies by 5, and then adds 10 to this total. Then the number of the ring-bearing finger across the two hands is counted and added (starting with the left little finger as 1), and the value is multiplied by 10. Finally, a number for the knuckle joint is added on, 1 for the joint nearest the hand, 3 for the tip joint. This gives a final total.

"When this number is announced," Fibonacci says, "it is easy to pinpoint the ring."

Can you see how?

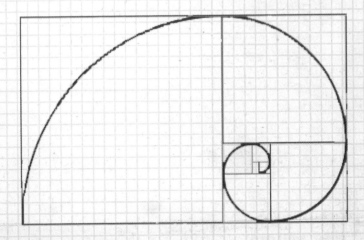

Solution on page 165

A CURIOUS THOUGHT

It has been said that the ultimate in exclusivity would be to build a house which possessed windows facing south on each of its four sides.

Does this seem a reasonable proposition?

Solution on page 165

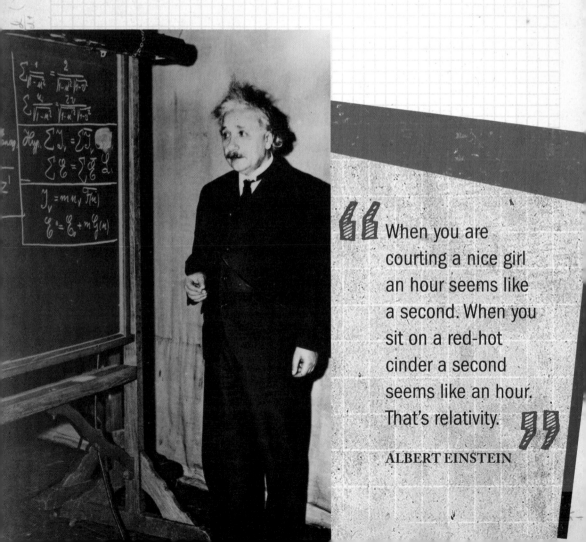

> When you are courting a nice girl an hour seems like a second. When you sit on a red-hot cinder a second seems like an hour. That's relativity.

ALBERT EINSTEIN

GOLD STANDARD

This question may seem laughable at first glance. I assure you, however, that I have no intention of making sport with you. Simplicity does not always indicate triviality.

Which is heavier – a 1-ton block of wood, or a 1-ton block of gold?

You may assume that both blocks are being weighed on the same weighing apparatus in the same terrestrial location, and that the machine is giving an identical value in both cases.

Solution on page 166

13
IN A SPIN

Thanks to the work of Copernicus, Galileo and many others, we know that the day happens because the world rotates on its axis, while the sun remains (apparently) still. But it is not always wise to blindly believe what you are told.

It would be reasonably straightforward to conduct an experiment that would prove that the Earth is revolving on its axis. You wouldn't even need to leave the Earth's surface.

Can you think of one?

Solution on page 167

SCIENTIFIC LOGIC

For this trial, no knowledge of the world's workings is needed. Your ability to think logically is the only thing being tested.

Five scientists from different Ivy League universities were engaged in a cutting-edge space programme. From the information provided, can you say which town the Irish scientist lived in?

The scientist in New Haven studied astrophysics, and she was not the American, who was called Emily. The British scientist lived in Cambridge, and was neither Marianne nor Sophie. The physics specialist was not named Jennifer or Alice. Providence was home to the scientist who studied metamaterials. Hanover was not home to the Canadian scientist. Alice, an Australian, was not studying astrophysics. Marianne studied biochemistry, and was not Irish. One of the scientists was studying nanotechnology. One of the scientists lived in New York.

Name	Nationality	Town	Speciality

Solution on page 168

AN EXPERIMENT

Now for a little practical experiment – one that you, dear reader, are able to take part in without any undue effort. Exhale slowly and steadily onto the palm of your hand. Make a mental note of how it feels. Now purse your lips, and blow vigorously onto your palm. You may use the other hand, if you wish.

You will observe that when breathing slowly, the air feels warm, but while blowing firmly, the air feels cool.

Your breath has not changed temperature. Neither has your hand. So why is there a difference?

Solution on page 168

> The true sign of intelligence is not knowledge but imagination.
>
> **ALBERT EINSTEIN**

A BIT OF POLISH

You will most likely have noticed that polished floors are considerably more slippery than rough (or fluffy) ones. So should it not follow that smooth ice is more slippery than bumpy ice? If you ever have occasion to pull a sledge, however, you will discover that it moves much more easily over uneven ice than over smooth ice. You may also have observed that roughened ice is trickier to walk on than glossy ice.

Why do you think that is?

Solution on page 169

TRIBAL MATHEMATICS

During the nineteenth century, a European colonel in Ethiopia recorded a report of an encounter with local tribesmen, from whom he was purchasing cattle. He wanted seven beasts, at a cost of 22 birr each. Not being numerate, the herder called a local priest to verify the total price.

When he arrived, the priest dug two parallel columns of holes. The right-hand column represented the purchase price, so in the first hole he placed 22 stones, and then halved the number of stones for each subsequent hole, rounding down. This gave him 22, 11, 5, 2 and 1 stone. The left-hand column then represented the cattle, and in its first hole he placed seven small stones. He then doubled the number of stones for each subsequent hole in the column, so that the holes contained 7, 14, 28, 56 and 112 stones.

Declaring even values to be evil, the priest then went down the right-hand column, and whenever he encountered an even number of stones – the 22 and 2 holes, in this instance – he removed the stones from both that hole and its neighbour in the left-hand column. Finally, he gathered up the stones remaining in the left-hand column – 14, 28, and 112 respectively – into one pile, which he counted out one by one. They came to 154 birr, which was indeed 22x7.

Indeed, this technique of multiplication will always work for whole numbers. But why?

Solution on page 169

18

PROBLEM IN GLASS

Imagine that you have a square window, five feet high, set in an opaque wall. That window lets in a certain amount of the available light outside. Simple.

It is possible to modify the window to precisely halve the amount of light that it lets in without changing the type of glass, placing a curtain, filter, shutter or any other sort of obstruction over the window or between the window and the viewer – while still keeping the window square, and five feet high.

Not so simple. Can you say how?

Solution on page 170

MASHED QUOTE

The puzzle below holds a well-known quotation. Although the words in each line remain in the correct order, all punctuation has been removed, and the lines themselves have been jumbled up.

Are you able to piece the original quotation back together?

> A FISH BY ITS
> ALBERT EINSTEIN
> THAT IT IS STUPID
> ABILITY TO CLIMB A TREE
> IT WILL LIVE ITS
> EVERYBODY IS A GENIUS
> BUT IF YOU JUDGE
> WHOLE LIFE BELIEVING

Solution on page 170

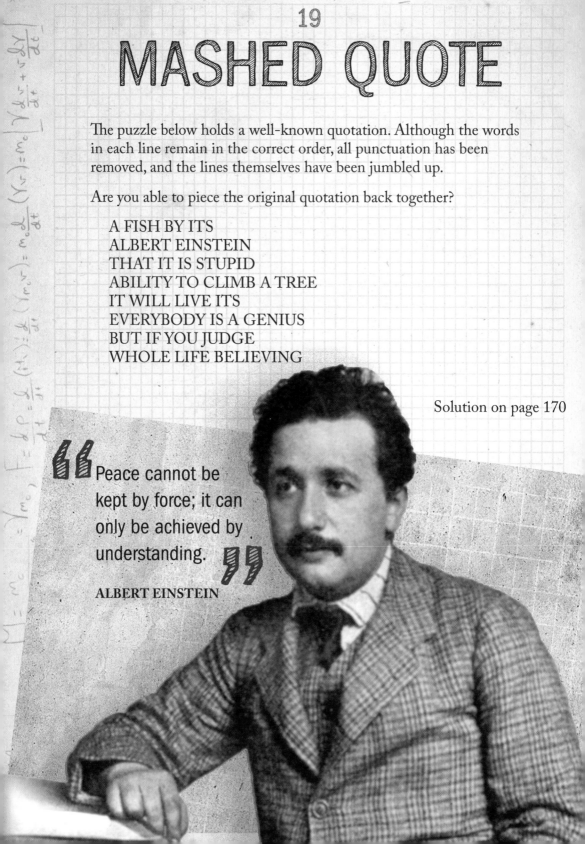

" Peace cannot be kept by force; it can only be achieved by understanding. "

ALBERT EINSTEIN

CIPHERTEXT

In this puzzle, the challenge is to decrypt a quotation that has been made obscure by the use of a simple cipher. Are you able to work out what it says?

JG ZPV XBOU ZPVS DIJMESFO UP CF

JOUFMMJHFOU SFBE UIFN GBJSZ UBMFT

JG ZPV XBOU UIFN UP CF NPSF

JOUFMMJHFOU SFBE UIFN NPSF GBJSZ UBMFT

Solution on page 171

INFINITE WORLDS

The mathematics of infinity can be startlingly beautiful. It can also be just plain startling.

Consider the natural numbers – 1, 2, 3, 4, etc. They are infinite; any number you can conceive of can be increased. Now, consider the even natural numbers – 2, 4, 6, 8, etc. These also obviously extend to infinity.

So if you compare the set of all natural numbers with the set of all even natural numbers, which is larger?

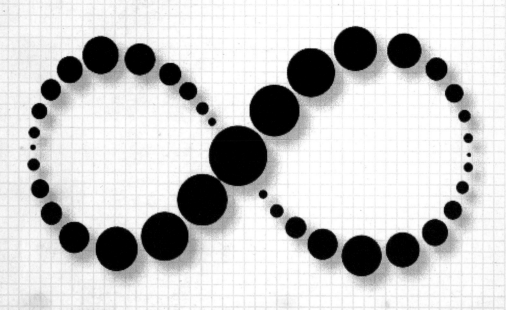

Solution on page 171

22
SUNLIGHT

Although we are 93 million miles from the sun, light travels so swiftly that it takes just eight minutes for its light to reach our Earth. To give you an idea about the vastness of our solar system, it takes sunlight 43 minutes to reach Jupiter, and up to nearly seven hours to get out to poor Pluto. But for now, return your thoughts to this planet.

For the sake of argument, let us pretend that where you are right now, sunrise tomorrow will occur at exactly 6 a.m. However, some unknowable force interferes overnight, so that the light of the sun reaches the Earth almost instantly. Perhaps a wondrous portal opens that effectively cuts the travel distance of the light down to under a second. The precise mechanism does not matter. What is important is that the light's journey is shortened from eight minutes to fractions of a second, without any ill effect to us.

What time would you then expect to see tomorrow's dawn?

Solution on page 172

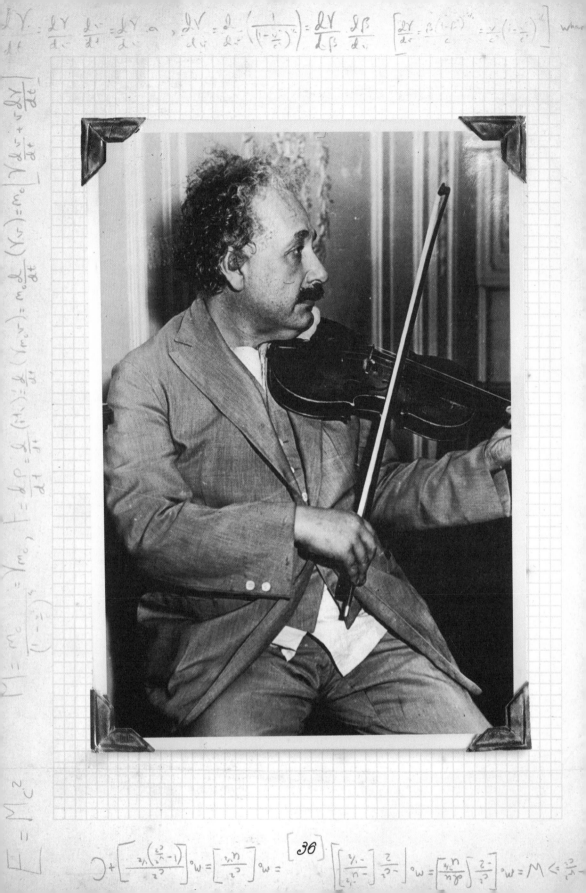

23
COFFEE CONNUNDRUM

Your ability to think logically is the only thing being tested in this trial.

Five friends are in a café, discussing their musical tastes. Using the information given below, can you find the name of the espresso drinker?

Steve is drinking cocoa, but he is not the person who likes rock, who is wearing red. The latte drinker is wearing black, and does not like pop or classical. One person is wearing green. Bruce is not drinking cappuccino. Megan is not drinking cappuccino either, and she doesn't like rock. Tea is being drunk by the country fan, who is not wearing cream. Diana likes electronica. Joan is wearing blue, and does not like country or classical.

Name	Drink	Music	Colour

Solution on page 172

$$R_{\mu\nu} - \tfrac{1}{2} g_{\mu\nu} R + g_{\mu\nu}\Lambda = \frac{8\pi G}{c^4} T_{\mu\nu} \qquad D = \mu k_B T \qquad T_c = \left(\frac{n}{\zeta(3/2)}\right)^{2/3} \frac{2\pi\hbar^2}{m k_B} \approx 3.3125$$

$$\ddot{a}_A = \sum_{B \neq A} \frac{G m_B \ddot{r}_{BA}}{r^2_{AB}} + \frac{1}{c^2} \sum_{B \neq A} \frac{G m_B \ddot{r}_{BA}}{r^2_{AB}} \left[v_A^2 + 2 v^2_B - 4 (\vec{v}_A \cdot \vec{v}_B) - \tfrac{3}{2}(\vec{n}_{AB} \cdot \vec{v}_B)^2 \right]$$

CHAPTER TWO

"I believe in intuition and inspiration. Imagination is more important than knowledge. For knowledge is limited, whereas imagination embraces the entire world, stimulating progress, giving birth to evolution. It is, strictly speaking, a real factor in scientific research."

ALBERT EINSTEIN

$$C_V = \left(\frac{\partial U}{\partial T}\right)_V$$

$$R_{\mu\nu} - \tfrac{1}{2} g_{\mu\nu} R + g_{\mu\nu}\Lambda = \frac{8\pi G}{c^4} T_{\mu\nu}$$

$$\frac{\delta L_G}{\delta g} - \tfrac{1}{2} P_{ab} = 0$$

$$\sum_{B \neq A} \frac{r^2_{AB}}{G m_B \ddot{r}_{BA}} + \frac{1}{c^2} \sum_{B \neq A} \frac{r^2_{AB}}{G m_B \ddot{r}_{BA}}$$

$$\left[v_A^2 + 2 v^2_B - 4 (\vec{v}_A \cdot \vec{v}_B) - \tfrac{3}{2}(\vec{n}_{AB} \cdot \vec{v}_B)^2 \right]$$

$$\frac{G m_B}{r_{AB}} \left[\vec{n}_{AB}(4 \vec{v}_A - 3\vec{v}_B)\right](\vec{v}_A - \vec{v}_B)$$

$$C_V = \left(\frac{\partial U}{\partial T}\right)_V$$

$$[\vec{n}_{AB}(4\vec{v}_A - 3\vec{v}_B)](\vec{v}_A - \vec{v}_B) \qquad -\tfrac{1}{2}\rho$$

MIRROR, MIRROR

Mirrors are a near-inevitable part of daily life. For most of us, they are indispensible. So, for such a simple object, a simple question.

Is an entirely clean mirrored surface visible?

Solution on page 176

THE EIGHT QUEENS

Max Bezzel, a German chess master, was the first to pose this question, in 1848. It has provided plenty of material for discussion since then.

A chess queen attacks in eight directions – vertical, horizontal and diagonal straight lines. His question was whether it was possible to place eight queens on a regular 8×8 chess board so that none of them could attack any other.

Are you able to find a way to do it?

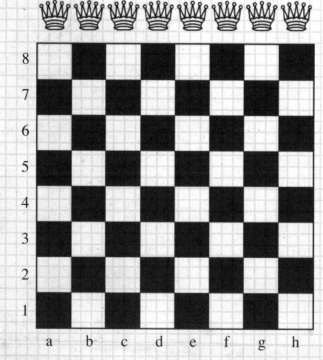

Solution on page 177

ABSOLUTELY TRUE

Several statements are given below. You may assume – for the duration of this problem – that they are absolutely true in all particulars. From that assumption, you should be able to provide an answer to the question that follows.

Animals that do not kick are always placid.

Donkeys have no horns.

A buffalo can always knock you over a gate.

No animals that kick are easy to stroke.

No hornless animal can knock you over a gate.

Only buffaloes are placid.

Are donkeys easy to stroke?

Solution on page 178

27
ELEVATING

The first elevator machine is believed to have been the invention of Archimedes, in the third century BC. It took the form of a rudimentary cab supported by a hemp rope, and powered by the manual labour of humans or animals. It wasn't until 1852 that Elisha Otis devised his safety elevator, designed to lock in place by toothed guides at the side of the wall, if it started moving too quickly. He demonstrated the principle at Crystal Palace in 1853, on an open platform above a stage, set between two toothed girders.

Most modern elevators are derived from his designs – but unlike his demonstration, they are enclosed within shafts. Though this is primarily for convenience, what safety benefit does a well-fitted shaft offer that a securely enclosed cab does not?

Solution on page 178

A QUESTION OF DISPLACEMENT

It is hopefully clear that a floating boat displaces a volume of water, and that the weight of the boat is equal to the weight of the water it displaces. Obviously, then, placing a boat into a partly filled tank of water means that the level of the water will rise. It therefore follows that if you place a lead weight into the boat, the water level will rise further.

So what will happen if you then drop that same lead weight over the side of the boat, into the water? Will the water level rise, fall or stay the same?

Solution on page 179

IMITATION OF REALITY

Motion pictures are a wonderful entertainment, but we should never forget that they provide an imitation of reality, rather than a reliable model. There are many possible examples of this to choose from, but let us select one of the simpler ones.

It is comparatively common, in movies, to see some unfortunate character fall from a cliff or very high building. This fate is invariably accompanied by a long scream of terror, which gets steadily fainter as the doomed victim plummets away. What is the error commonly encountered with this sound effect?

Solution on page 180

TRIAL BY LOGIC

For this trial, no knowledge of the world's workings is needed. Your ability to think logically is the only thing being tested.

A collection of sales reps find themselves stuck in an airport en route to separate business meetings. From the information below, can you say what goods the company Power Projects sell?

C. A. F. are based in either Holland or Portugal, and their rep is travelling to either Frankfurt or Paris. The Power Projects rep is travelling to either Barcelona or Prague. The Belgian company sells either designer equipment or robotics. The film camera company is either TekTrex or 3ird Eye, and is either Portugese or Belgian. The company that sells protective gear is sending a rep to either Prague or Frankfurt. The rep who is travelling to Glasgow sells either robotics or leatherwear. Karma's rep is travelling to either Barcelona or Frankfurt, is based in either Portugal or Italy, and sells either protective gear or designer equipment. 3ird Eye's rep is travelling to Glasgow or Frankfurt, and either sells film cameras or protective gear. There is a company that is based in Denmark.

Company	Location	Destination	Goods

Solution on page 181

SITTING COMFORTABLY

Try sitting straight on a chair, with your back and lower legs vertical, and your thighs horizontal. You will discover that if you neither move your feet nor bend your torso forwards, it is impossible to stand up. Feel free to try it. You will be unable to stand until you either move your feet back, or your chest forwards.

Why is that?

Solution on page 182

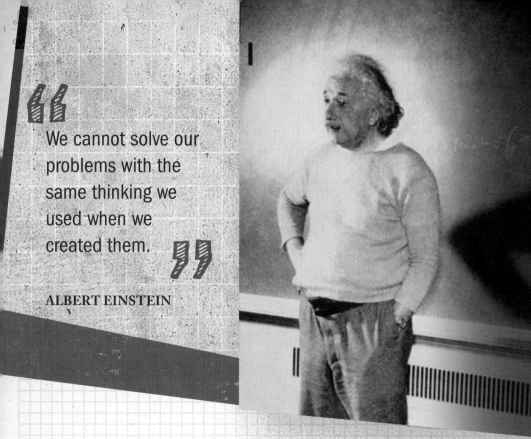

32

BAREFOOT DOCTOR

It is likely that you have walked around a cold house barefoot at some time or another in your life. If so, you will probably have noticed that under such conditions, carpeted flooring feels warmer to walk on than tile.

It should be clear that this is the case even when there is absolutely no difference between the actual temperatures of the various stretches of flooring. So why do we perceive such a difference?

Solution on page 183

CIPHERTEXT

In this puzzle, the challenge is to decrypt a quotation that has been made obscure by the use of a simple cipher. Are you able to work out what it says?

ERUSSERP EVAW FO NOITAIRAV A SA YN

OHPMYS NEVOHTEEB A DEBIRCSED UOY F

I SA GNINAEM TUOHTIW EB DLUOW TI E

SNES ON EKAM DLUOW TI TUB YLLACIFI

TNEICS GNIHTYREVE EBIRCSED OT ELBI

SSOP EB DLUOW TI

Solution on page 183

34

BALL DROP

This puzzle may require a certain amount of thought.

Imagine that you have a pair of perfectly elastic balls, one very much larger and heavier than the other. You place the lighter ball on top of the heavier one, and then drop them a distance of 1ft onto a perfectly rigid floor.

How high will the lighter ball bounce?

It may help to bear in mind that kinetic energy is:
(mass x (speed x speed)) / 2.

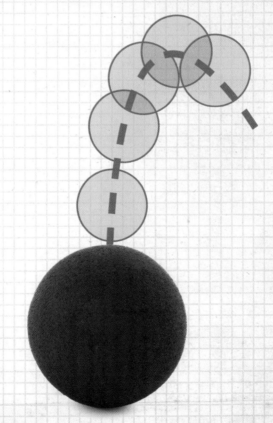

Solution on page 184

PENDULUM

A pendulum is a very simple machine, but a highly interesting one none the less. A pair of identical pendulums suspended in a vacuum jar will, naturally enough, move in perfect synchrony once set swinging. If you lengthen the string of one of the pair, it will slow down, falling behind the other. Similarly, if you instead shortened the string, it would speed up.

What would happen if you kept the strings the same length, and instead replaced one of the weights with a similarly sized bob made of a substantially lighter material?

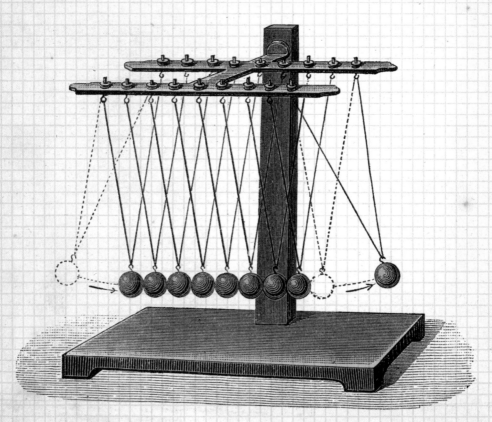

Solution on page 185

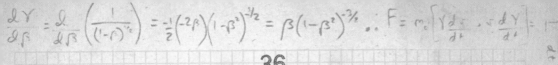

TRUE IN ALL PARTICULARS

Several statements are given below. You may assume – for the duration of this problem – that they are absolutely true in all particulars. From that assumption, you should be able to provide an answer to the question that follows.

No one goes to a party without brushing his or her hair.

Untidy people are never fascinating.

Alcoholics have no self-control.

People with brushed hair look fascinating.

No one wears white gloves, unless he or she is going to a party.

A person is always untidy, if he or she has no self-control.

Do alcoholics wear white gloves?

Solution on page 185

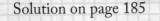

FERMI'S PARADOX

Somehow, physics genius Enrico Fermi is best-known nowadays for a light-hearted luncheon question he asked some colleagues at the Los Alamos National Laboratory: "Where are they?"

With hundreds of trillions of stars visible to us, there could well be vast numbers of alien civilizations out there, many in our own galaxy. The Sun is a fairly young star as these things go, so there could well be civilizations billions of years old, again in our galaxy. Why haven't they colonized it completely? Why can't we see evidence of their activities? Why aren't they buzzing through the skies on a daily basis?

Both religious thinkers and skeptics have cited Fermi's Paradox as proof that there is no such thing as intelligent extraterrestrial life. However, the apparent paradox is founded on a large number of assumptions, any of which might well be false. Fermi himself didn't consider the question to be anything other than a casual basis for a discussion. It's certainly no evidence for the non-existence of alien life.

How many of the Paradox's unfounded assumptions can you think of?

Solution on page 186

> There is no difference between large and small problems, for issues concerning the treatment of people are all the same.

ALBERT EINSTEIN

OVERFLOW

This is another experiment that you can easily try for yourself. Fill a wineglass up to the very brim with water. Now, get some pins or needles. Carefully add them to the glass one by one by poking the sharp tip gently straight down into the water, and letting go.

The glass is full, so how many pins do you think you would be able to add without the water spilling out? One or two? As many as ten, perhaps? Why?

Solution on page 187

GRAVITY

It can be difficult to believe that the weight of an object makes no difference to how quickly gravity pulls it downwards. This is not usually our experience. Light objects in daily use often fall more slowly than heavy ones. We can pluck a falling sheet of paper out of the air, but a full mug of coffee is far harder to rescue. But the reality is that gravity acts on every molecule of an object simultaneously, so it doesn't matter how much mass it has. Every speck of substance gets accelerated downwards at the same speed.

Can you think of a simple household experiment to prove the truth of the matter?

Solution on page 188

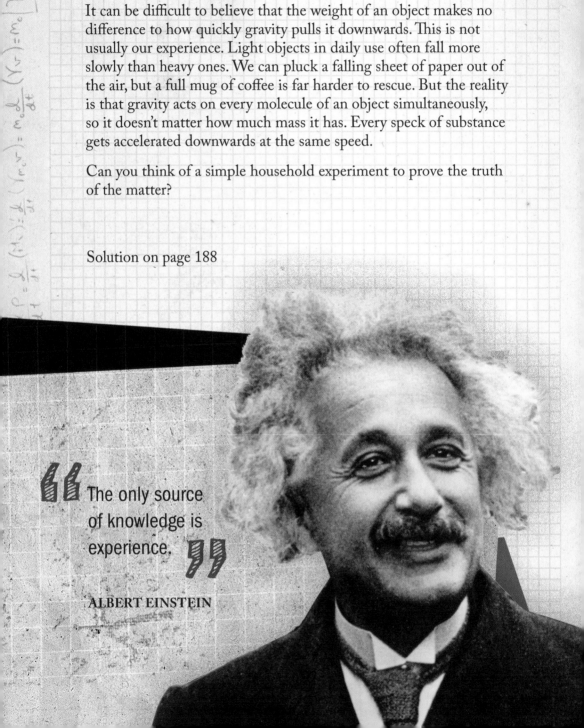

The only source of knowledge is experience.

ALBERT EINSTEIN

COSTLY LOGIC

Are you able to unravel this test of logic?

A party of friends each ordered different main courses and side dishes at a restaurant, and each of their meals cost a different sum. Can you say whose meal was the most expensive?

Antonia paid more than the diner who had a duck breast. The diner who ordered fricassee of spinach paid less than the diner who wanted creamed leeks – which did not accompany the fillet of beef. Either Lucille ate the fillet of beef and Burt had a ratatouille Provencal, or Antonia ate the fillet of beef and Lucille had the ratatouille Provencal. Neal, who had wild mushroom risotto, paid 50p more than the diner who had rump of lamb, who was either Calvin or Antonia. The rump of lamb cost more than the twice-roasted pork belly. Either Calvin or Antonia paid £25.50 and had creamed leeks. Someone had glazed carrots. None of the diners ate a vegetarian meal. The amounts paid for the meals were £24.00, £24.50, £25.00, £25.50 and £26.00. There was a diner named Burt. Someone ate venison loin.

Diner	Main Course	Side Dish	Cost

Solution on page 189

MARBLES

While they may not be the universally beloved toy that they were in the past, marbles are still delightful and intriguing things.

Let us say that you have a bag of marbles. You may assume, for the sake of this exercise, that the marbles stay where they're put, and that they are all the same size. If you place one on a flat floor, how many will you be able to fit around it so that they are all touching both the floor and the central marble?

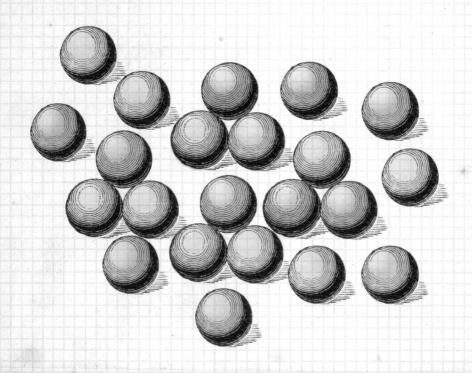

Solution on page 189

GOING DOWN

Imagine that it is the first day of August, and you are standing in a pleasant European woodland glade. It is a warm, sunny day. All around you, nature goes about its summery business.

What season of the year is it, three metres below the surface of the ground?

Solution on page 190

EXERCISE FOR THE MIND

Several statements are given below. You may assume – for the duration of this problem – that they are absolutely true in all particulars. From that assumption, you should be able to provide an answer to the question that follows.

No husband who often buys presents for his wife can be considered difficult.

A methodical husband always returns home in time for dinner.

A husband who hangs his hat on the tap is never well-housetrained by his wife.

A well-housetrained husband often buys presents for his wife.

No husband can fail to be difficult, if his wife does not keep him well-housetrained.

Only unmethodical husbands always hang their hat on the tap.

Are well-housetrained husbands in time for dinner?

Solution on page 190

CROCODILE CONUNDRUM

The ancient Greeks possessed an interesting riddle of unknown provenance. You may find it diverting.

In the riddle, a hungry crocodile snatched a baby from its unwary mother on the banks of a river. The mother begged for the baby's safe return. Not wanting to look cruel in the eyes of the gods, the crocodile agreed to give her a chance. It said to her, "If you correctly predict the fate of your baby, then I will return him. Otherwise, I will eat him." The crocodile did not want to return the baby, of course.

What can the mother say to get her baby safely returned?

Solution on page 191

HOT METAL

It is well-known that metal expands when it is heated. The precise amount of the expansion varies according to both metal and temperature, but it can be quite significant – as any structural engineer can attest.

So. Imagine a simple, circular piece of iron, with a hole at its centre. The iron is put into a hot fire. As the metal expands, does the hole become larger or smaller?

Solution on page 191

A JOURNEY BY TRAIN

Momentum can be as stern a jailer as mathematics, trapping the unwary into an unassailable prison of causality. To put it another way, any action you take will remove some possibilities from your future, while opening others.

Imagine a pair of trains, starting at opposite ends of a stretch of straight, level parallel track. It may help to imagine a city at each terminus, if this idea seems a little to abstract. As Train 1 sets out from City A to City B, Train 2 sets out from City B to City A.

When they pass by each other, Train 1 has one hour left to complete its journey to B, while Train 2, which is slower, has four hours remaining before it reaches A. Assuming that their speeds are constant throughout their journey, how many times faster is Train 1 than Train 2?

Solution on page 192

CIPHERTEXT

In this puzzle, the challenge is to decrypt a quotation that has been made obscure by the use of a simple cipher. Are you able to work out what it says?

```
UREBVFZ NG PBZZNAQ FRAFRYRFF OEHGNYVGL

QRCYBENOYR YBIR BS PBHAGEL NAQ NYY GUR YBNGUFBZR

ABAFRAFR GUNG TBRF OL GUR ANZR BS CNGEVBGVFZ UBJ

IVBYRAGYL V UNGR NYY GUVF UBJ QRFCVPNOYR NAQ

VTABOYR JNE VF V JBHYQ ENGURE OR GBEA GB FUERQF

GUNA OR CNEG BS FB ONFR NA NPGVBA VG VF ZL

PBAIVPGVBA GUNG XVYYVAT HAQRE GUR PYBNX BS JNE

VF ABGUVAT OHG NA NPG BS ZHEQRE
```

Solution on page 192

POWER

Setting aside the use of tools – such as levers – can you say which regular movement is the most powerful one that a human body is capable of?

Solution on page 193

CHAPTER THREE

"Great spirits have always encountered opposition from mediocre minds. The mediocre mind is incapable of understanding the man who refuses to bow blindly to conventional prejudices and chooses instead to express his opinions courageously and honestly."

ALBERT EINSTEIN

$$R_{\mu\nu} - \tfrac{1}{2} g_{\mu\nu} R + g_{\mu\nu} \Lambda = \frac{8\pi G}{c^4} T_{\mu\nu}$$

$$D = \mu k_B T$$

$$T_c = \left(\frac{n}{\zeta(3/2)}\right)^{2/3} \frac{2\pi \hbar^2}{m k_B} \approx 3.3125$$

$$\vec{a}_A = \sum_{B \neq A} \frac{G m_B \pi \vec{r}_{BA}}{r^2 AB}$$

$$C_V = \left(\frac{\partial U}{\partial T}\right)_V$$

$$+ \frac{1}{c^2} \sum_{B \neq A} \frac{G m_B \pi \vec{r}_{BA}}{r^2 AB} \left[v_A^2 + 2 v^2 B - 4(\vec{v}_A \cdot v_b) - \tfrac{3}{2}(\vec{r}_{AB} \cdot \vec{v}_b)^2 \frac{G m_B [\vec{r}_{AB} (4\vec{v}_A - 3\vec{v}_b)](\vec{r}_A - \vec{v}_b)}{r^2 AB} \right.$$

$$R_{\mu\nu} - \tfrac{1}{2} g_{\mu\nu} R + g_{\mu\nu} \Lambda = 8\pi \frac{G}{c^4} T_{\mu\nu}$$

$$R_{\mu\nu} - \tfrac{1}{2} g_{\mu\nu} R + g_{\mu\nu} \Lambda = \frac{\delta\sqrt{G}}{\delta g^g} - \tfrac{1}{2} P_{ab} = 0$$

$$+ \frac{1}{c^2} \sum_{B \neq A} \frac{r^2 AB}{G m_B \pi \vec{r}_{BA}}$$

$$\frac{r^2 AB}{r^2 AB}$$

$$\left[v_A^2 + 2 v^2 B - 4(\vec{v}_A \cdot v_b) - \tfrac{3}{2}(\vec{r}_{AB} \cdot \vec{v}_b)^2 \right]$$

$$[66]$$

$$[\vec{r}_{AB} (4\vec{v}_A - 3\vec{v}_b)](\vec{r}_A - \vec{v}_b)$$

$$- \tfrac{1}{2} P$$

$$C_V = \left(\frac{\partial U}{\partial T}\right)_V$$

MAGIC SQUARE

The German artist Albrecht Dürer was vital to the spread of the Renaissance into northern Europe, and made many huge contributions to artistic theory. In one of his best-known and most enigmatic artworks, entitled *Melencolia I*, he placed a prominent magic square, reproduced below.

It is a superlative example of a magic square, highly sophisticated in many ways. Like most of its kind, the horizontal rows, vertical columns and diagonal lines in Dürer's Square all add up to a common number, in this instance 34. But there are more methods to get to totals of 34 as well.

How many different ways can you find to divide Dürer's Square into four sets of four numbers, each set totalling 34?

16	3	2	13
5	10	11	8
9	6	7	12
4	15	14	1

Solution on page 196

SILVER SPOON

It is common, when pouring hot tea into a glass, to put a teaspoon into the glass first. Ideally, the spoon should be silver. This is done to ensure that the glass does not crack.

But why is there a risk it might?

Solution on page 197

ART AND LOGIC

For this trial, no knowledge of the world's workings is needed. Your ability to think logically is the only thing being tested.

Several people were visiting art galleries in different cities in search of works from different schools of art, but each was impressed by something a little outside their usual tastes. From the information given below, can you say which artist's work impressed James?

The person looking for cityscapes went to a gallery in Toronto, and was neither Kara nor Pippa. The person at the Oxford gallery was impressed by a Newman piece, and was not Adam, who was looking for Pre-Raphaelite works. The person who was impressed by a Haring piece went to a gallery in Madrid. Sebastian was looking for Op art, and was not impressed by a Newman piece. The person who was impressed by a Barker work was neither James nor Sebastian. The person looking for Cubism did not go to New York. Kara was impressed by a Riley work, and was not looking for Neoclassical pieces. One person was impressed by a Rosing piece. One person went to a gallery in Frankfurt.

Person	City	Looking For	Impressed by

Solution on page 197

BATHTIME

We have established that things expand when heated. You may well have observed that it can be difficult to put on a boot or firm shoe after a hot bath or shower. So has expansion due to heat made the cells in your foot larger?

Solution on page 198

PROBABILITY PARADOX

Probability can turn up some interesting wrinkles, particularly when it comes to interconnections amongst an group. This is especially true when it comes to common birthdays. Now, you need to assemble a group of 367 random people to have a 100% chance that two of them will share the same birthday (allowing for 29 February). So how many do you need for a 99% chance that two were born on the same day? What about a 50% chance?

Solution on page 199

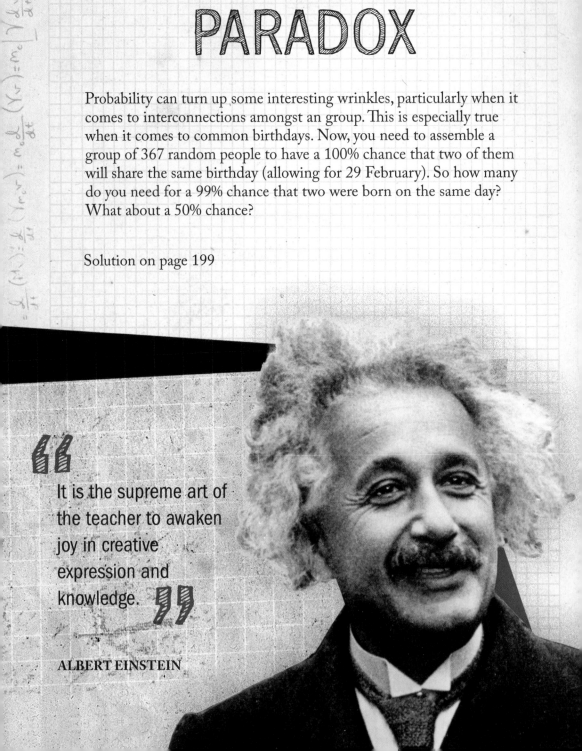

> It is the supreme art of the teacher to awaken joy in creative expression and knowledge.

ALBERT EINSTEIN

ABSOLUTELY TRUE

Several statements are given below. You may assume – for the duration of this problem – that they are absolutely true in all particulars. From that assumption, you should be able to provide an answer to the question that follows.

Everything that is not ugly may be kept in a main room.

Nothing encrusted with salt is ever quite dry.

Nothing should be kept in a main room, unless it is free from damp.

Deck chairs are always kept near the sea.

Nothing that is made of mother-of-pearl can be ugly.

Whatever is kept near the sea gets encrusted with salt.

Can deck chairs be made of mother-of-pearl?

$$R_{\mu\nu} - \frac{1}{2} g_{\mu\nu} R + g_{\mu\nu} \Lambda = \frac{8\pi G}{c^4} T_{\mu\nu}$$

$$\vec{a} A = \sum_{B \neq A} \qquad T_c = \left(\frac{n}{\zeta(3/2)}\right)^{2/3} \frac{2\pi \hbar^2}{m k_B} \approx 3.3125$$

Solution on page 199

TWILIGHT

From time to time, when the weather conditions are correct, it is possible to see the sun's rays streaking across the sky from behind an obstruction, such as a mountain, or a hole in clouds. They invariably fan out from a point just behind the obstruction. Rays of these sort are called "crepuscular rays" by meteorologists.

When light strikes the Earth's atmosphere, it is all parallel, every beam moving in exactly the same direction. So how can a hole in clouds, or the peak of a mountain, cause them to diverge?

Solution on page 200

> If A is success in life, then $A = x + y + z$. Work is x, play is y and z is keeping your mouth shut.
>
> **ALBERT EINSTEIN**

ON THE BOIL

Have you ever paid attention when boiling a kettle of water? It may not seem a particularly edifying or fascinating procedure, but although it is entirely commonplace in our modern world, it remains a marvel none the less. Of particular interest for the purposes of our exercise is the pattern of sound involved in the process. When you initially start hearting the water, the kettle is silent. However, it is not long before a faint crackling and hissing noise starts. As time progresses, the noise gets steadily louder, becoming a noticeable bubbling. This bubbling grows in strength, but then suddenly drops dramatically. A moment later, the kettle fully boils.

Why the sudden drop in volume?

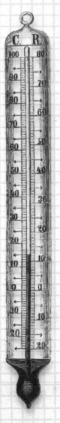

Solution on page 201

WOOLLY PROBLEM

Can you overcome this tricky question of logic?

Five members of a knitting circle are all working on different projects, using wool of different colours, for different purposes. Can you say which item of clothing is made from indigo wool?

The person knitting with red wool is making socks, but not for a spouse or lover. The person who is using blue wool is knitting for a friend, but is not making a blanket. Someone is knitting a sweater. Radka is neither using grey wool, nor is she knitting for a neighbour. One person is using indigo wool. Kristen is using mauve wool, but she is not knitting something for a neighbour – that person is making a scarf. Hope is not knitting with grey wool. Ebony has a niece to make a present for. Delmer is making a hat, but not for a spouse.

Person	Wool Colour	Project	Purpose

Solution on page 201

58
THE ILLUSIONIST

Imagine a conjurer's trick. You are in the audience, watching a magician at work. She shows you a bare wooden table, with nothing on it and nothing beneath it. With a flourish, she places an empty, open box upside-down on the table. When she whips it away again, the disembodied head of her lovely assistant is there, moustaches bristling. He proceeds to answer some questions she puts, grinning out at the audience as he does so.

This trick can be easily constructed using just principles already established in this book. Can you see how?

Solution on page 202

TAN LINES

It may seem counterintuitive, but there is a significant difference between attempting to get a suntan at a sandy beach, and attempting to do the same thing in your garden. This is true even if your garden happens to be on the very edge of the beach in question, and even if you do not enter the water.

Can you think why it might be so?

Solution on page 203

CIPHERTEXT

In this puzzle, the challenge is to decrypt a quotation that has been made obscure by the use of a simple cipher. Are you able to work out what it says?

GSV NLHG YVZFGRUFO GSRMT DV XZM VCKVIRVMXV

RH GSV NBHGVIRLFH RG RH GSV HLFIXV LU ZOO

GIFV ZIG ZMW ZOO HXRVMXV SV GL DSLN GSRH

VNLGRLM RH Z HGIZMTVI DSL XZM ML OLMTVI

KZFHV GL DLMWVI ZMW HGZMW IZKG RM ZDV

RH ZH TLLW ZH WVZW SRH VBVH ZIV XOLHVW

Solution on page 204

61
THE PRISONER'S DILEMMA

One of the more interesting thought experiments deriving from Game Theory, the Prisoner's Dilemma has been attracting considerable thought and discussion ever since its inception.

A pair of criminals are separated, and offered the same deal – testify against your acquaintance and go free, ensuring he receives ten years in jail. If both testify against each other, both will be jailed for five years. If both refuse, both will be jailed for just six months.

No communication of any form is possible between the two. They are not close friends, and do not know for certain what the other will choose – but they do not dislike each other, and would rather spend the least amount of time possible in prison.

If you were one of the two prisoners, what would be your best course of action?

Solution on page 204

62
LAMPLIGHT

In earlier years, before electric lamps were convenient, miners used a very particular form of illumination. Known as a Davy Lamp, these devices were oil-burning lamps enclosed in a very fine mesh. If the miner entered a low-oxygen environment, the lamp would go out. More importantly, if he encountered a pocket of flammable gases, it would not cause an explosion – unlike a more normal lamp.

Why not?

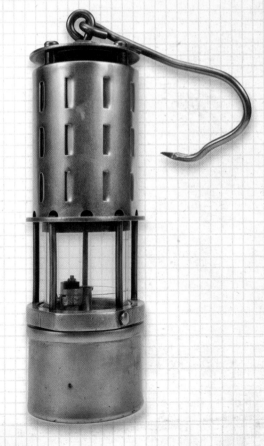

Solution on page 205

STATEMENT OF FACT

Several statements are given below. You may assume – for the duration of this problem – that they are absolutely true in all particulars. From that assumption, you should be able to provide an answer to the question that follows.

No day is unlucky, when Robinson is pleasant to me.

Wednesdays are always cloudy.

When people take umbrellas, the day is never dry.

Robinson is only unpleasant to me on Wednesdays.

Everybody takes their umbrella with them when it is raining.

My lucky days are always dry.

Are rainy days cloudy?

Solution on page 205

SEQUENCES

Pattern-matching is one of humanity's greatest skills. When we encounter a new object, our minds decide how to deal with that item by putting it into as many different categories as possible – colour, details of shape, texture, context, scent, noise, etc. Once the raw data has been turned into labels, that complete set of labels is matched against the pattern of other sets of labels, to find what type of known object is the best match. Our skill at this sort of pattern identification is so great that even the most powerful computers are still significantly inferior to human observation at certain types of visual processing tasks.

These sequence puzzles will test your abilities at matching data patterns. There is a very specific reason for the following sequence of letters. Can you figure it out, and find the next one in the list?

T F S E T T F ...?

ABCDEFG
HIJKLMN
OPQRSTU
VWXYZ

Solution on page 206

SUNLIGHT

Imagine that it is a cold, clear winter's day. The sun is bright, but there is deep snow on the ground. You are in a wide open space, with several smallish squares of cloth – the same size, but dyed in the colours of the rainbow, along with black and white. Being curious, you lay them out on the snow, in a line, not touching each other, and go about your business.

When you return to the cloth pieces, after several hours of sunshine, what would you expect to find?

Solution on page 206

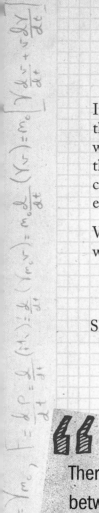

> There is no difference between large and small problems, for issues concerning the treatment of people are all the same.

ALBERT EINSTEIN

BICYCLE
REVOLUTIONS

A modern bicycle typically has wheels of equal size. However, if you attach a counter that measures revolutions to both front and back wheels, you will find that over the course of a few weeks of typical usage, the front wheel will have a higher revolution count that the rear wheel.

Why is that?

Solution on page 208

PRESENT LOGIC

For this trial, no knowledge of the world's workings is needed.
Your ability to think logically is the only thing being tested.

Five men have purchased birthday presents for their wives. From
the information given below, can you say how long the woman
receiving the fur has been married?

One of the men is named Len. Of the five couples, Randolph and
Eunice got married directly before the man who bought the necklace.
Mercedes is getting a book. One couple have been married seven years,
another just three years. The man who bought the bracelet has been
married 16 years. He is not Jeffrey. Michael bought a fur coat. Terrell
has been married for 14 years, but not to Anita. Elisha has been
married for five years. Irma is not getting a necklace or lingerie, and
she is not married to Michael.

Man	Wife	Years Married	Present

Solution on page 209

THE SANDS OF TIME

Picture, if you will, an hourglass. When you turn it over, the sand flows downwards into the bottom compartment. The sand that is descending is quite clearly in free fall. So does that mean that the hourglass is very slightly lighter?

Solution on page 209

THE COIN CHALLENGE

This is another problem which can easily be turned into a diverting demonstration for your friends. Take a large plate, and lay a thin coin on it, ideally not on the centre. Then add enough water to cover the top of the coin. The challenge is to pick up the coin with your uncovered fingers without getting them wet, and without moving or tipping the plate.

Can you see how it is done?

Solution on page 210

IS THAT A OF FACT?

You may assume – for the duration of this problem – that these statements are absolutely true in all particulars. From that assumption, you should be able to provide an answer to the question that follows.

No shark is ever not well turned out.

A fish that cannot dance a minuet is contemptible.

No fish is well turned out unless it has three rows of teeth.

All fishes, except sharks, are kind to children.

No heavy fish can dance a minuet.

A fish with three rows of teeth is never contemptible.

Are heavy fish kind to children?

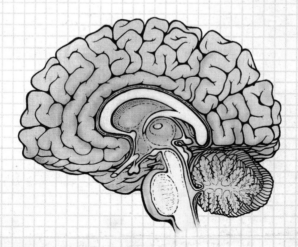

Solution on page 211

RAVENS

Time for some deductive reasoning. Carl Hempel, a towering philosopher of science, created a curious paradox based on logical deduction. It goes as follows:

Assume for this exercise that all ravens are black. That implies that anything which is not black is not a raven. We can support the assumption by looking at my pet raven, Nevermore, which is black. We can support the implication by looking at this green apple, which is not a raven.

Therefore, seeing a green apple proves that all ravens are black.

What's the problem in the logic here?

Solution on page 211

SHOOTING STARS

If you were in the habit of watching the sky at night, you would be able to observe that it is considerably easier to spot meteors between midnight and dawn than it is to do so between dusk and midnight. Why do you imagine that to be the case?

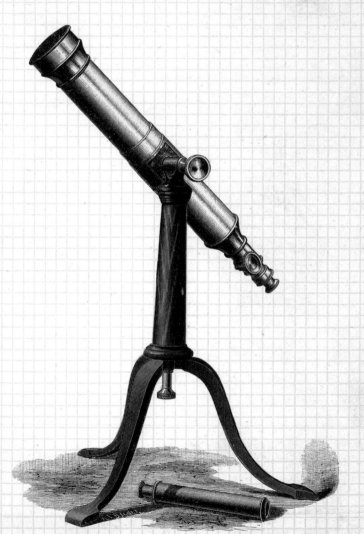

Solution on page 212

SIMPLICITY

Just a quick, simple question this time.

By what proportion does four fourths exceed three fourths?

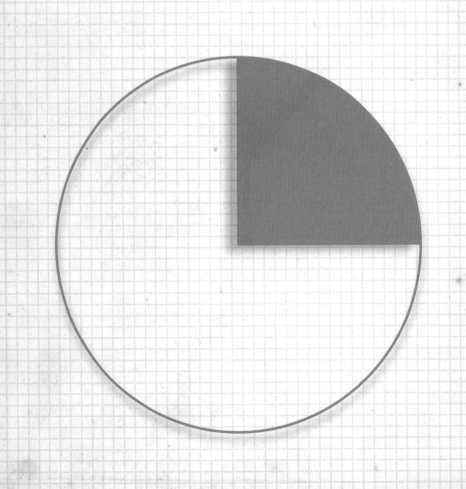

Solution on page 212

74
CIPHERTEXT

In this puzzle, the challenge is to decrypt a quotation that has been made obscure by the use of a simple cipher. Are you able to work out what it says?

HIQJHI UXJPBW FYDRQJ QJRKWV ETHIFY UXHIDR

WVHIGU RKUXGU HIVCWV UXRKBW HIGULS WVFYDR

QJRKQJ OGBWET HIFYKA DRQJJP HIGUIO UXRKPH

RKQJHI IORKUX PHWVRK DRQJRK WVKAHI UXXYXY

Solution on page 213

THAT'S NO MOON...

Suppose that one day it becomes possible to hollow out an asteroid and turn it into a space station. For now, let's assume the unlikely case where such an asteroid is a perfect, unblemished, non-rotating sphere, and that its outer wall is uniformly thick.

In the absence of any artificial gravity, would an object released inside the asteroid be pulled towards its centre or towards the nearest point on the shell, or would it remain where it was?

Solution on page 213

THE FLY

Imagine that there are a pair of trains heading directly towards each other on the same piece of track. They are 100km apart, and each is travelling at 50km per hour. At this same instant, a fly leaves the windscreen of one train, and flies directly to the other, at an extremely impressive speed of 75km/h. As soon as it reaches the other train, it reverses its direction. It keeps doing so, right until the two trains collide.

How far does the fly travel?

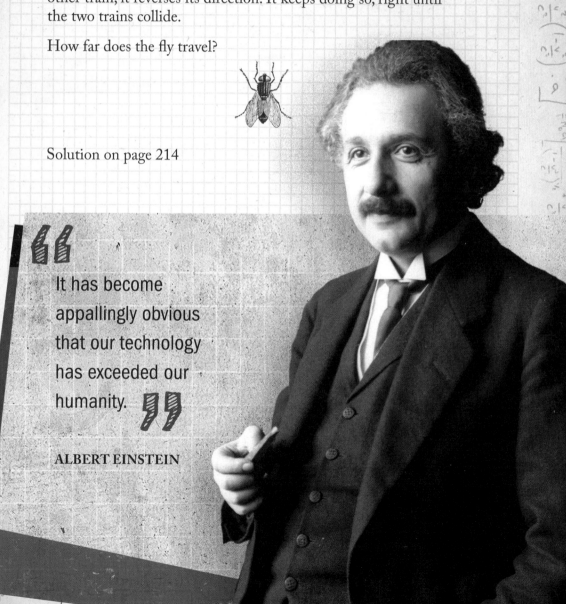

Solution on page 214

> It has become appallingly obvious that our technology has exceeded our humanity.

ALBERT EINSTEIN

UP IN SMOKE

If you were to light an unfiltered cigarette and place it on a matchbox or similar small object – a less easy proposition, in these modern times – you would observe that smoke comes out of both ends. However, at one end it rises, while at the other end it sinks. Why is that, do you think?

Solution on page 214

THINK LOGICALLY

For this trial, no knowledge of the world's workings is needed. Your ability to think logically is the only thing being tested.

A group of drivers are delivering their cargoes. Can you figure out which city is receiving beef?

The grey truck is being driven to Cambridge. One cargo is travelling in a white truck. The milk cartons are in a blue truck, but are not delivered by James or Delmer. Omar is delivering flour, but not to Birmingham. The cargo for Manchester is not being driven by Krista or Omar. One cargo is going to York. The Birmingham cargo, in a green truck, is not apples (which are being delivered by Isaac). The beef is not in a red truck. James is going to Andover, but not with rice.

Driver	Cargo	City	Truck Colour

Solution on page 215

CHAPTER FOUR

"Although I am a typical loner in my daily life, my awareness of belonging to the invisible community of those who strive for truth, beauty, and justice has prevented me from feelings of isolation."

ALBERT EINSTEIN

COOLING OFF

Most of our mechanical day-to-day conventions have developed because they are enduringly effective. We mix ingredients in a bowl because the lack of seams makes it easier to ensure an even mixture, and because we still need a reasonably large vessel to minimize spillage. Most locks turn clockwise, because that motion is easier for right-handers, who make up the bulk of the population. And, when heating a saucepan, we put the pan directly over the heat source, rather than a long way above it, or off to the side, because that is the best way to maximize heat transfer. So what would you do for cooling? Imagine you had a closed metal box which you wanted to cool using a slab of ice that you are not willing to break. What would be the most effective method of cooling the box?

Solution on page 218

NEEDLEPOINT

It's a rather astounding fact, but if you gather a bunch of needles of length r, and toss them randomly (rather than placing them carefully) onto a surface divided into parallel strips whose width is also equal to r, you can calculate pi. (You can do this with needles of a different length to the strip width, but the mathematics becomes more complicated.)

Specifically, pi turns out to be 2 x the number of needles you toss / the number of tosses in which a needle crosses a seam between strips. In other words, the probability that a needle will land crossing a seam is 2/pi.

How does pi come into it?

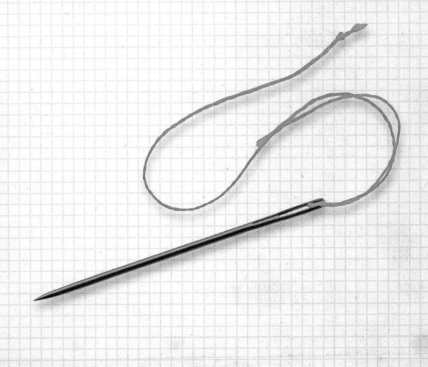

Solution on page 218

THE SWEET TRUTH

Several statements are given below. You may assume – for the duration of this problem – that they are absolutely true in all particulars. From that assumption, you should be able to provide an answer to the question that follows.

All humans – except valets – have at least some common sense.

No one who lives on candy can be anything but a mere baby.

Only hopscotch players know what real happiness is.

No mere baby has any common sense.

No driver ever plays hopscotch.

No valet is ignorant of what true happiness is.

Do drivers live on candy?

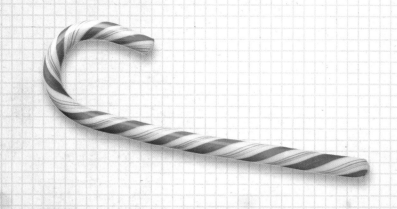

Solution on page 218

$$\frac{d\gamma}{d\beta} = \frac{d}{d\beta}\left(\frac{1}{(1-\beta^2)^{\frac{1}{2}}}\right) = -\frac{1}{2}(-2\beta)(1-\beta^2)^{-\frac{3}{2}} = \beta(1-\beta^2)^{-\frac{3}{2}} \therefore F = m_o\left[\gamma\frac{d\dot{z}}{dt} + \dot{z}\frac{d\gamma}{dt}\right] =$$

RISING UP

There is much fascinating knowledge to glean from the mechanics of flotation, and their application. We have come a very long way from Archimedes' apocryphal bathtub Eureka moment, to the point where we are able to send submersible vehicles into the very deepest crevices of the Earth – and even get them back again afterwards, unharmed. At the bottom of the Mariana trench, some 11km below the surface, the pressure of the water is an incredible 1000 times greater than atmospheric pressure, almost 16,000 pounds of force per square inch of exposed surface.

For now, however, we must turn our attention to shallower waters. Picture, if you would, a small boat floating in a swimming pool. You are standing on the edge of the pool, with a brick. You can either toss the brick into the boat – which will not sink as a result – or directly into the pool.

Which choice will make the pool's water level rise more?

Solution on page 219

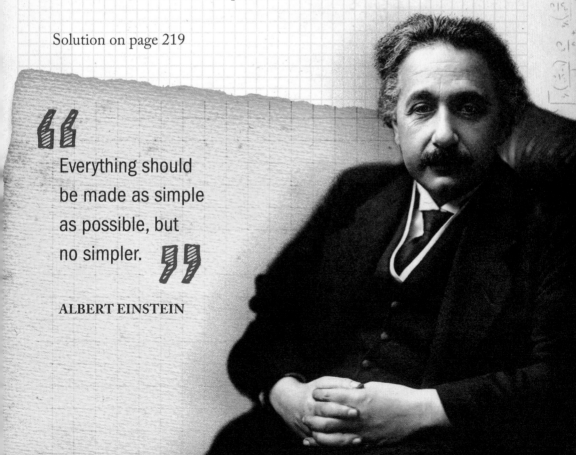

> Everything should
> be made as simple
> as possible, but
> no simpler.

ALBERT EINSTEIN

83

BARREL

This is not as directly practical a question as it would have been a century or two ago, but the principles are nicely illustrative.

So, imagine that you have a barrel. It is large and open-topped, and contains some water. Looking in, you can guess that it's somewhere around half-full. In the absence of any tool that would allow you to measure the water, can you figure out how to tell whether it is more or less than half-full?

Solution on page 219

RISING CHIMP

Imagine that there is an even rope of negligible weight draped over a wheel, which permits it to slide perfectly freely. Equal lengths of the rope descend from either side. On the left side, the rope ends in a 10kg weight. On the other side, perfectly level with the weight, is a young chimp, also weighing 10kg.

When you give a signal, the chimp will start climbing the rope. Which of the two, the chimp or the weight, will reach the top first?

Solution on page 220

LOGIC PUZZLE

For this trial, no knowledge of the world's workings is needed. Your ability to think logically is the only thing being tested.

Several women are taking taxi journeys across New York for various purposes. From the information given below, can you say where the client visit took place?

Kathleen paid more for her journey than the woman who went out to survey property. Either Annie or Kathleen went out to see a client, paying $5 more than the woman who went to a board meeting. The woman going to Central Park paid less than the woman going to Grand Central Station, who was not on a photographic assignment. One of the women went to Liberty Island. Either Virginia went to SoHo and Kathleen was on a photographic assignment, or Robin went to SoHo and Virginia was on a photographic assignment. The fares were $60, $65, $70, $75 and $80. Marcella, who went to 54th and Lexington, paid $5 more than the woman who went out to see a client. Either Kathleen or Annie went talent-scouting and paid $75 for the ride.

Woman	Destination	Purpose	Fare

Solution on page 220

DRAUGHTS

On a cold day, you may have noticed an unpleasant draught coming from your window, even if it is firmly shut and there are no cracks anywhere. This is perfectly natural, and no fault of your window or its maker. Can you say why it occurs?

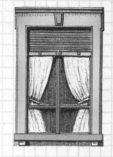

Solution on page 221

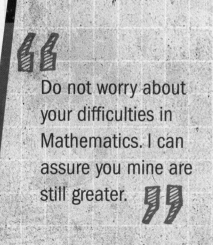

> Do not worry about your difficulties in Mathematics. I can assure you mine are still greater.

ALBERT EINSTEIN

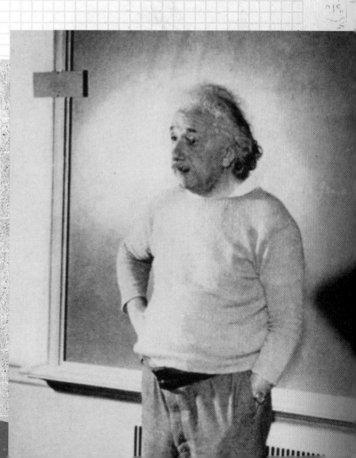

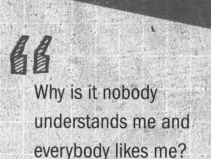
87

SALT

For quite some time, it has been a relatively common practice in households to add a few grains of rice to a salt cellar or shaker. This is not done to change the flavour of the salt, and typically this rice is not consumed. Even if a little of the rice should somehow accidentally end up on a dish, it will be removed and discarded. So, clearly, the addition of the rice is not a matter of taste, either flavours or aesthetics. Why, then, is this done?

Solution on page 222

88
CIPHERTEXT

In this puzzle, the challenge is to decrypt a quotation that has been made obscure by the use of a simple cipher. Are you able to work out what it says?

```
YWZZO  OHXQF  UWZBN  HBNHX  ADQUK  VVLIY
EUKRG  TQDQF  ORGZO  LBNRG  EXATZ  AOLVO
RSOSE  NWHXQ  TDRGU  HKHXG  ERLVV  RLDQS
UHSHR  LGLVQ  EFWZH  SXGRE  OWBNW  FZKIH
TXWZK  HILVQ  EFJUV  GLBNR  AGXTG  MRLVG
ERQFW  AZGRR  NGWZK  DIDQQ  TFEWB  HNWZK
EIHXR  NGQFH  YXVLB  ONRGX  UTGRL  HVGRV
ALRGW  VZKIU  EKRGZ  TORGI  OYIYW  PZKIH
LXEWR  AGZOO  YSLVQ  BFHXV  ELVLD  TQLVO
TSDQZ  EODQB  RNIYU  TZZNK  HYVNJ  ADIIQ
NOKNC  AEDVN  NQRRG  YDPYL  BRSHY  OZIQW
DPCWW  YUZGH  EHYSW  LDRVW  SCRZW  EAGFX
```

Solution on page 222

ZENO'S RACECOURSE

With his Dichotomy paradox, the Greek philosopher Zeno of Elea states that movement ought to be impossible. Any motion made has to pass through a halfway point before it arrives at its goal. But then that halfway point becomes a new goal, and it too has a halfway spot, and so on. In fact, even the tiniest movement has an infinite number of ever-smaller halfways that must be first achieved, and no finite amount of time would ever be enough to hit them all.

Clearly, movement is possible, and there is a logical error in the Dichotomy. Can you see what it is?

Solution on page 223

EGG IN A BOTTLE

It is possible to get a fresh, uncooked egg, still in its undamaged shell, into a bottle whose neck is too small to admit it. There is no trick involved with the bottle's construction, and neither is the egg in any way unusual. Can you imagine how such a thing might be achieved?

Solution on page 225

EXERCISE IN LOGIC

Several statements are given below. You may assume – for the duration of this problem – that they are absolutely true in all particulars. From that assumption, you should be able to provide an answer to the question that follows.

I trust every animal that belongs to me.

Dogs gnaw bones.

I let no animals into my study unless they will beg when told to do so.

All the animals in the yard are mine.

I admit every animal that I trust into my study.

The only animals that are willing to beg when told to do so are dogs.

Do all the animals in the yard gnaw bones?

Solution on page 226

$$\frac{d\gamma}{d\beta} = \frac{d}{d\beta}\left(\frac{1}{(1-r)^{1/2}}\right) = -\frac{1}{2}(-2\beta)(1-\beta^2)^{-1/2} = \beta(1-\beta^2)^{-3/2} \therefore F = m_c\left[\frac{\gamma d_s}{dt} + v\frac{d\gamma}{dt}\right] =$$

BERTRAND'S BOX

Joseph Bertrand, a nineteenth-century French mathematician, created an enduring probability question now known as Bertrand's Box. The premise is quite simple. Imagine that you have three identical boxes. Each contains two coins, of identical shape, but in one box both coins are gold, in another both are silver, and in the third, there is one of each metal.

The boxes are mixed up, and you are given a coin at random from one of them. That coin is made of gold. Can you say what the chance is that the other coin in the same box is also gold?

Solution on page 226

“Only two things are infinite, the universe and human stupidity, and I'm not sure about the former. **”**

ALBERT EINSTEIN

WARM THOUGHTS

If you wrap a thermometer in a thick wool coat and leave it for a period of time, it will not heat up. Yet if you wrap yourself in the same thick wool coat, it will indeed warm you up. How come?

Solution on page 227

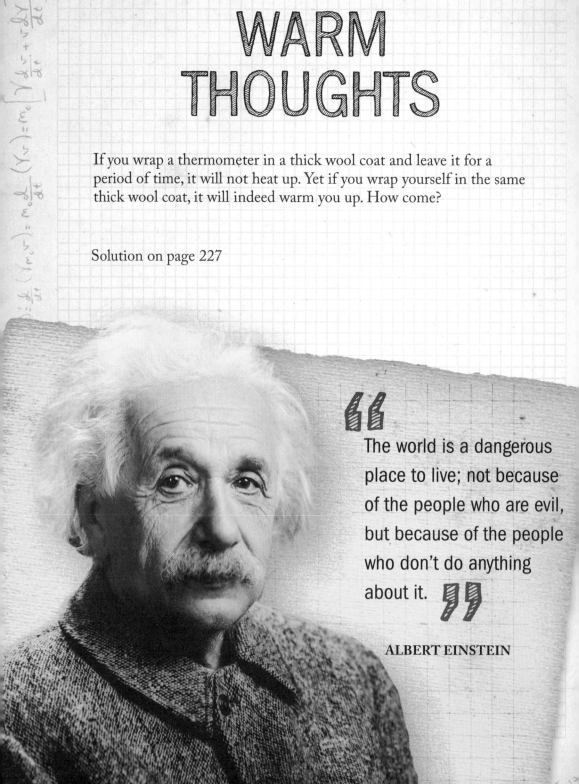

> The world is a dangerous place to live; not because of the people who are evil, but because of the people who don't do anything about it.

ALBERT EINSTEIN

CHIAROSCURO

Now that we have the darkness thoroughly tamed in our homes and streets, there is an undeniable romance to the night. The familiar is made strange by the changes in illumination and the lack of detail, and every shadowed nook and cranny holds the promise of new discovery. To walk at night is to be drawn back to childhood, when the world was less certain, and new marvels seemed to be an inevitability. So imagine, if you will, that it is evening, and you are walking along a level street lit by a solitary streetlight. As you walk past the light and away from it, your shadow is cast ahead of you, plain for you to see. How fast does the top of your shadow move compared to your own pace if the street light is twice your height?

Solution on page 227

TESTING TRIAL

For this trial, no knowledge of the world's workings is needed. Your ability to think logically is the only thing being tested.

Five people went on long-distance trips, with a range of travelling partners. From the information given below, can you say who visited the Antarctic, and with whom?

Taylor went to Mauritius or Japan with either a colleague or a parent. Felicia went on holiday with either a cousin or a friend. The Argentinean destination was either a lodge or a city. The villa was either in Japan or Argentina, and either Lindsey or Lorrie went there. The outpost was visited either with a friend or a colleague. The person staying at either the hotel or the lodge was with a sibling. Yolanda went to either Japan or Iceland with either a cousin or a colleague, and stayed in either an outpost or a city. Lorrie stayed in either an outpost or a villa, and went with either a sibling or a colleague.

Person	Location	Type of Place	Partner

Solution on page 228

GOLF BALLS

When we think of golf balls, we imagine bright, dimpled balls covered in a hard layer of polyurethane. But the materials are constantly being revised and updated, and the dimples were first put into production balls in 1905. Until the middle of the nineteenth century, golf balls were made from (roughly) spherical leather pouches stuffed with boiled feathers. These became obsolete in 1848, when the Rev Dr Paterson discovered that the sap of the sapodilla tree could be heated into a suitably resilient sphere. His "gutties" quickly replaced the old "featheries". But it wasn't until the twentieth century that players discovered that a dimpled ball could travel as much as four times as far as an undimpled but otherwise identical one, and they became the standard.

Why do the dimples make such a difference?

Solution on page 228

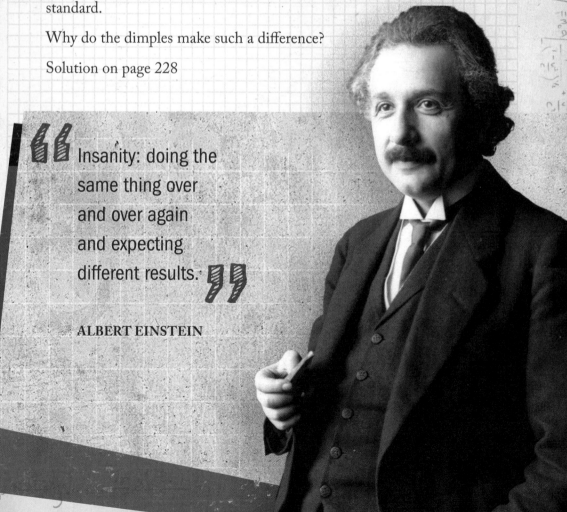

> Insanity: doing the same thing over and over again and expecting different results.

ALBERT EINSTEIN

LEAPING FROM A MOVING BUS

Firstly, it needs to be said that one should never attempt to jump from a moving vehicle. It's potentially fatal, and if other options exist, they should be taken.

With that said, let us suppose that for some hideous reason, you need to leap from a bus while it is driving along at its normal speed. Assuming no bollards, trees, pedestrians or other obstacles to slam into, what is the best direction in which to jump?

Solution on page 229

ANIMAL LOGIC

Several statements are given below. You may assume – for the duration of this problem – that they are absolutely true in all particulars. From that assumption, you should be able to provide an answer to the question that follows.

Animals are always mortally offended if I fail to notice them.

The only animals that belong to me are in that field.

No animal can guess a conundrum, unless it has been properly trained in a school.

None of the animals in that field are badgers.

When an animal is mortally offended, it always rushes about wildly and howls.

I never notice any animal, unless it belongs to me.

No animal that has been properly trained in a school ever rushes about wildly and howls.

Can badgers solve conundrums?

Solution on page 230

ZENO'S STADIUM

In another paradoxical thought exercise, Zeno suggested the following situation. There are two lines of five runners, all moving at the same speed, running around and around a track. One group is moving clockwise, and the other is moving anticlockwise. They are being observed by a line of five watchers, stationary. Each line of five people is the same length.

The two lines of runners meet as they are passing the spectators. In the time that the head of the clockwise runners passes the entire line of anticlockwise runners, the head of the anticlockwise runners will pass just half the line of the spectators. However, as ascertained already, both sets of runners are moving at the same pace.

Zeno asserts that this means the anticlockwise runners need twice as long to cover the same distance as the clockwise runners, even though they're moving at the same speed. This is impossible, and thus, he derives, time is illusionary.

Is there anything to his argument?

$$R_{\mu\nu} - \frac{1}{2} g_{\mu\nu} R + g_{\mu\nu} \Lambda = \frac{8 \pi G}{c^4} T_{\mu\nu}$$

$$\vec{a} A = \sum_{B \neq A} \qquad T_c = \left(\frac{n}{\zeta(3/2)}\right)^{2/3} \frac{2\pi \hbar^2}{m k_B} \approx 3.3125$$

$$\frac{G m_B \hat{\pi} BA}{r^2 AB} + \frac{1}{c^2} \sum_{B \neq A} \frac{G m_B \hat{\pi} BA}{r^2 AB}$$

Solution on page 231

100
BUBBLES

Let us venture now into realms of pure speculation. Imagine that the universe we know was somehow completely obliterated. In all the infinite vastnesses of space, nothing remains but two equal spheres of water, unfathomable distances apart. With nothing else whatsoever in existence, these two spheres would inevitably be pulled towards each other by their respective gravities. The process would be incredibly slow but, eventually, the two spheres would come together. With me so far? Now, reverse the situation. The entire universe is filled with an infinite reservoir of pure, equally dense water. There is nothing else – save for two spherical bubbles of fresh Earth air, again unfathomably far apart. How would the bubbles move, if at all?

Solution on page 231

PERFECT OVAL

So many trivial modern tasks would have been incredible wonders in the distant past. Now, it is a moment's work to construct a geometric circle so perfect that it would make an ancient craftsman weep. The earliest compasses we know of come from the Nuragic people, a Bronze Age civilization from the island of Sardinia, somewhere in the region of 1500 BC. Three-and-a-half thousand years later, a perfect circle is notable only in passing. All you need is some paper, a pair of compasses and a pencil.

How would you use the same tools to construct a geometrical oval?

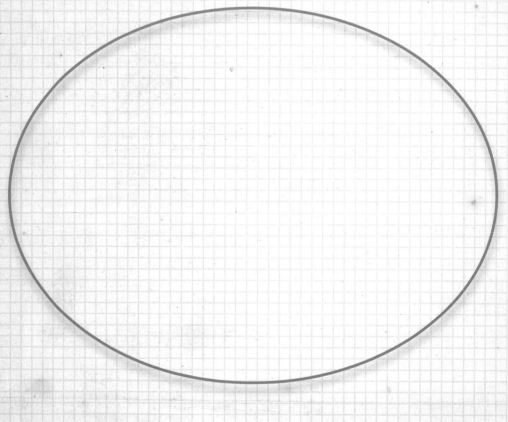

Solution on page 232

102
CIPHERTEXT

In this puzzle, the challenge is to decrypt a quotation that has been made obscure by the use of a simple cipher. Are you able to work out what it says?

```
96472 85697 66953 12949 27917

96455 13335 11633 75941 57593

33319 44511 17594 15154 69153

55933 45331 95451 39298 55662

85569 34186 33447 28569 77964

53529 35691 53559 33117 28129

14175 94151 54759 41575 93345

33195 28129 14115 50000
```

Solution on page 233

103
IMPOSSIBLE THINGS

Imagine for a moment that you cut a playing card in two and placed the halves on top of each other. You then repeated this, cutting the two half-cards in two, and forming a stack of four pieces. Repeating this process, you continued until you had cut a total of 52 times.

Do you imagine that the resulting pile would be more or less than a mile high? By how much?

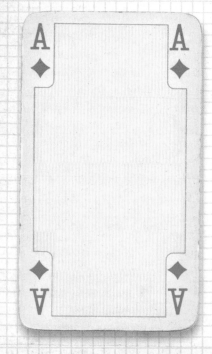

Solution on page 233

SCHRÖDINGER'S CAT

Erwin Schrödinger's famous thought experiment has become one of the most famous formulations of quantum mechanics, the theory underpinning modern understanding of the universe. It is quite simple in its principle.

Imagine that there is a cat in a steel chamber, along with a machine that will release a poisonous gas when a small bit of radioactive material decays – a process which is as close to truly random as we can find. There is no way to observe the cat, or to know whether the machine has triggered or not. Over the course of any given hour, there is a 50% chance that the material will decay and the cat will be poisoned.

After an hour, what state is the cat in?

Solution on page 234

SCALES

There are many assumptions we take for granted when it comes to measuring our weight. Generally, we are so keen to ensure it has not increased that any other considerations are totally banished from our minds. Few of us stop to really wonder what our weight actually signifies, in terms of the physics underlying reality. Most people spend their entire lives in locations which have broadly the same relationship to the planet. So there is no real need to worry about distance from the centre of the Earth, or atmospheric pressure, or the relationship between weight and mass. But scales are surprisingly sensitive to all sorts of conditions, not just the cosmic. To get an accurate reading from a set of weighing scales, you must stand on them, straight, without moving. If you bend down, the scales will underestimate your weight. Why is this?

Solution on page 235

THINK LOGICALLY

For this trial, no knowledge of the world's workings is needed. Your ability to think logically is the only thing being tested.

Five children are unwell. From the information below, can you say which illness and treat were the fate of the child with yellow pyjamas?

The child in red pyjamas got a book as a treat. The child with measles (not Billie or Frankie) got given a toy. Alexis has mumps. A different child (in green pyjamas) was visited by a friend who had already had his or her disease. One child was given jelly. Frankie was wearing orange pyjamas, and did not have tonsilitis. Lee had scarlet fever, and was not wearing green pyjamas. The child with chicken pox did not get ice cream. The child in blue pyjamas was neither Robin nor Lee.

Child	Illness	Treat	Pyjama Colour

Solution on page 236

WEIGHTY PROBLEM

Having previously alluded to the many and various assumptions we tend to unconsciously make regarding weight, it is now time to call such things to the forefront of your mind. Imagine, if you would, that you are in possession of a 1kg sphere of iron – where 1kg specifically means equal to the mass of the "International Prototype of the Kilogram", the physical object which, at time of printing, is the standard definition of what the unit "kg" means.

Now, stretch your imagination further by assuming that below the first couple of inches of topsoil, the substance of the earth has a perfectly constant density – that is, if you took out a cubic metre of matter from any two random spots beneath the earth's solid surface, both would be identical in mass. Given this even density, where would your spherical iron kilogram weigh the most? High up a mountain? Deep underground? Or somewhere else entirely?

Solution on page 237

"
A new type of thinking is essential if mankind is to survive and move toward higher levels. "

ALBERT EINSTEIN

ZENO'S ARROW

In his Arrow paradox, Zeno pointed out that an arrow at rest occupies a fixed area of space. In flight, it also occupies a certain fixed space. So, in any instant, the arrow is frozen. If it moved during that instant, you'd be able to split that instant into smaller, 'before' and 'after' moments. This showed, he asserted, that the arrow was in fact truly motionless, which meant that motion was either entirely illusionary, or happened between instants, outside time.

Was he wrong?

Solution on page 237

CHAPTER FIVE

"One of the strongest motives that lead men to art and science is escape from everyday life with its painful crudity and hopeless dreariness, from the fetters of one's own ever-shifting desires. A finely tempered nature longs to escape from the personal life into the world of objective perception and thought."

ALBERT EINSTEIN

TRUE STATEMENTS

Several statements are given below. You may assume – for the duration of this problem – that they are absolutely true in all particulars. From that assumption, you should be able to provide an answer to the question that follows.

I never put a cheque I receive on my file, unless I am anxious about it.

All the cheques I receive that are not marked with a cross are payable to bearer.

No cheques I receive are ever brought back to me, unless they have been dishonoured at the Bank.

All cheques I receive that are marked with a cross are for amounts of over £100.

All cheques I receive that are not on my file are marked "not negotiable".

No cheque of yours that I have received has ever been dishonoured.

I am never anxious about a cheque I receive, unless it should happen to be brought back to me.

None of the cheques I receive that are marked "not negotiable" are for amounts of over £100.

Are the cheques of yours that I have received payable to bearer?

Solution on page 240

SURVIVAL INSTINCT

Precarious circumstances often provide an excellent opportunity for consideration of the rules of the physical world, when taken as abstracts. In practise, of course, it's a different matter. When your life is in imminent danger, taking the time to admire the laws of nature is difficult. The survival instinct outweighs scientific curiosity in all but the most oblivious of devoted researchers.

For this example, imagine that you find yourself in a small boat, some distance from shore, without any supplies, or any oar, sail, fan or other means of propulsion. For reasons that I shall leave entirely to your imagination, you are unable or unwilling to have any physical contact with the water, so swimming and paddling are both out of the question. However, there is a rope tied to the bow at the boat's front-most point. If you take the other end of the rope and jerk on it sharply, will you propel the boat forwards?

Solution on page 240

THE HUNDRED

Consider the following, rather odd numerical statement:

123456789 = 100

You can make it accurate in several different ways by adding mathematical operators. For example, 1+2+3+4+5+6+7+(8x9)=100. In this instance, you need nine operators – a bracket pair, a multiplication sign and seven addition signs. But you can make do with less than nine operators to make the equation valid.

Note that you are allowed to use minus signs and division signs as well. You may also combine adjacent numbers into a single value – i.e., 2 and 3 become 23. Combination like this does not count as using an operator.

By following these rules, you can balance the equation with just three operators. Can you see how?

1234689

Solution on page 241

UNDER PRESSURE

We are often unaware of air pressure, except perhaps when it is unusually high, or when it contributes to unusual weather. It seems nonexistent to us most of the time, a sort of general neutral background that we may intellectually be aware of, but which has no actual force to it. We may notice air when the wind is blowing strongly, if it impedes our movement, or makes our trees sway. Usually, however, we think of it as both intangible and invisible, a sort of nothingness that provides the oxygen we need to stay alive.

However, this general assumption is completely wrong. Air is far heavier than we realize, and presses in on us continually. The peculiar truth is that we live, effectively, at the bottom of a vast reservoir of heavy gases, in much the same way as strange creatures live on the bottom of the deepest sea beds. From the point of view of a hypothetical space-dwelling creature, the Earth's surface and the ocean's depths would be almost equally forbidding. The atmospheric pressure on an average-sized human can exceed twelve tons of weight, and we bear these forces continually.

Why are we not instantly crushed?

Solution on page 241

PURE LOGIC

For this trial, no knowledge of the world's workings is needed. Your ability to think logically is the only thing being tested.

Several people at a farmer's market all made purchases from the artisanal egg farmer. From the information given below, can you work out how many eggs Bertha purchased, and what kind they were?

Megan wore black. Someone bought six goose eggs. The person in the cyan coat – not Byron – bought 15 eggs. Lou bought chicken eggs, and got three more eggs than the person in the yellow coat. Franklyn bought 12 eggs, which were not turkey eggs. The quail eggs were not bought by Megan, or by the persons in yellow or white coats. The person in magenta bought duck eggs. One person bought three eggs, and another one bought nine.

Person	Number of Eggs	Egg Type	Coat Colour

Solution on page 242

WATERLINE

Pop-pop boats were once considered highly popular toys for children. Some are still available nowadays, but in this modern age of remotely controlled vehicles, they are a curious throwback. They were generally made of metal before this age of plastics, brightly painted, and sized for use in a bath or small pond. Internally, pop-pop boats are very simple. They contain a small heater, positioned under a metal boiler, which in turn has an exhaust pipe. This pipe points out of the back, below the waterline. To get the boat to operate, one simply forces a little water up the exhaust and into the boiler, and lights the small burner underneath it. Once the device warms up, the boat will jet across the water in little bursts of acceleration. The noise it makes, a small popping sound, gives it its name.

Can you see how it works?

Solution on page 242

CIPHERTEXT

In this puzzle, the challenge is to decrypt a quotation that has been made obscure by the use of a simple cipher. Are you able to work out what it says?

VMFVE VIOBL FWRLZ GSCRM TGESL FTASR GXLZM

MVWEV IYAVP MLYDM YFSGG LBALF IHTVO UZTHP

BLRFI HVAOU SLCDB LFTDL FOSWZ XGMDV IVEZO

OGNSV DLOIO WOFLL PRLMT ZGOBL FZWMW ZXMGZ

XXOLI WRRMT OBAGS LNLZH JSIHD OPTIW KJYSZ

Solution on page 243

116
THE
GRAND HOTEL

In 1947, the mathematician George Gamow attributed his paradox of the Grand Hotel to the German mathematician David Hilbert, one of the most important mathematical thinkers of the early twentieth century.

In the paradox, the Grand Hotel has an infinitely large number of rooms, each of them occupied. Then an infinite coach-load of new guests turn up, demanding to be accommodated in separate rooms. The hotel's manager nods, and with a bit of shuffling, accommodates all the new arrivals, without having to ask any of the existing guests to either leave or share a room.

How?

Solution on page 243

SEQUENCES

These sequence puzzles will test your abilities at matching data patterns. There is a very specific reason for the following sequence of letters. Can you figure it out, and find the next one in the list?

A   D   G   J   M   ...?

ABCDEFG
HIJKLMN
OPQRSTU
VWXYZ

Solution on page 245

THINK LOGICALLY

Several statements are given below. You may assume – for the duration of this problem – that they are absolutely true in all particulars. From that assumption, you should be able to provide an answer to the question that follows.

All of the dated letters in this room are written on blue paper.

None of the letters in this room are in black ink, except those written in the third person.

I have not filed any of the letters in this room that I can read.

None of the letters in this room written on one sheet of paper are undated.

There is a precise overlap between crossed letters and black ink.

All of the letters in this room written by Brown begin with "Dear Sir".

All of the letters in this room written on blue paper are filed.

None of the letters in this room written on more than one sheet of paper are crossed.

None of the letters in this room that begin with "Dear Sir" are written in the third person.

Can I read Brown's letters?

Solution on page 246

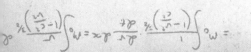

BERRY PARADOX

In 1927, the Welsh philosopher Bertrand Russell recorded a paradox devised by George Godfrey Berry, a librarian at Oxford University. Berry pointed out that there are only a limited number of words, so there was a hard limit on the number of possible phrases of up to 12 words in length. However, there were infinitely many whole numbers. That had to imply that there was a positive integer that was not definable in 12 words or less. However, that number could then be defined as "the smallest positive integer not definable in 12 words or less" – an 11-word definition.

The paradox, then is that there must be a smallest integer not definable in 12 words or less – but the very fact of it being that number means that it cannot actually be the smallest integer not definable in 12 words or less. Is there a resolution to the paradox?

Solution on page 246

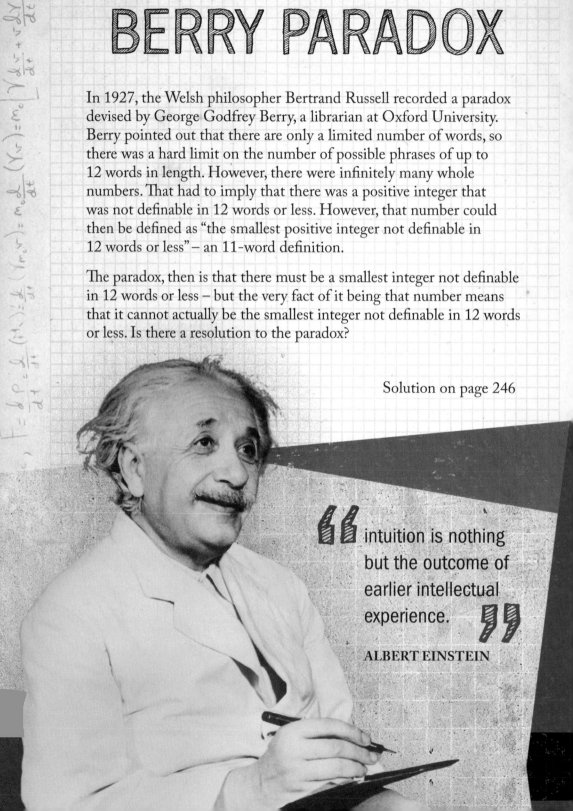

> intuition is nothing but the outcome of earlier intellectual experience.
>
> **ALBERT EINSTEIN**

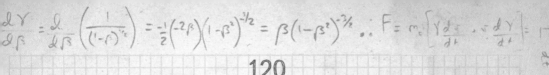

120
BALLISTICS

Imagine a hypothetical rifle, set up on a large, empty plain on Earth which has somehow become a vacuum. Gravity remains normal, though. With the rifle set up to aim at 45°, a bullet leaving the barrel at 620m/s would land nearly 40km away, having reached 10km in height.

How far do you imagine the bullet would get from the same rifle once the plain had returned to normal air density?

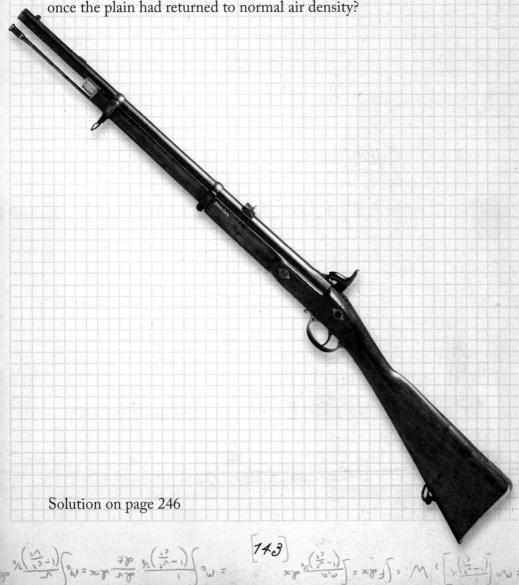

Solution on page 246

TIME AND TIDE

We are told that the tides of the ocean are caused primarily by the moon's gravitational pull on the Earth. But there are two high tides a day in many places, and if a spot on the Earth is at high tide, generally so is the location precisely on the opposite side of the planet. Water bulging up towards the moon because of gravity seems reasonable, but why is water also bulging up directly away from it?

Solution on page 247

> **As far as the laws of mathematics refer to reality, they are not certain; and as far as they are certain, they do not refer to reality.**
>
> **ALBERT EINSTEIN**

TRIAL BY LOGIC

For this trial, no knowledge of the world's workings is needed. Your ability to think logically is the only thing being tested.

Five people regularly run into each other in the refreshment area of their local meeting rooms. From the information given below, can you say who the tea-drinker is, and what they do there?

The person who is in a reading group likes to drink juice. Saldana drinks water. She does not like choc chip cookies. Someone is acting in a play. The person who likes ginger snaps is attending an art class. This is neither Saldana nor Nessa. Vilma likes butter biscuits, but doesn't drink soda. The person who eats garibaldi biscuits is not learning French. The person who likes coffee is not Tripp or Vilma. The person who is discussing metaphysics likes to drink soda. This is not Tristan, who likes digestives.

Person	Activity	Biscuit	Drink Type

Solution on page 247

THE DRIFT

There is something magical about the first arrival of snow each winter. You wake to discover that the whole world seems to have been transformed into something new and clean. There is as much wonder in it as in any of nature's sleights of hand. Consider, too, that it enables easy access to creative effort – it's as if everywhere you turn, there is a fresh supply of modelling clay that will not stick to your fingers. No wonder so many of us react with innocent delight.

If you live in an area where the snow drifts in winter, you will most likely have observed that by proportion, significantly more snow will accumulate against a telephone pole or hedge than against the side of a house nearby. Intuition would suggest the opposite – that the wall, being larger, would gather more snow than a thin pole.

Can you suggest why this is not the case?

Solution on page 248

LOGICAL ASSUMPTION

Several statements are given below. You may assume – for the duration of this problem – that they are absolutely true in all particulars. From that assumption, you should be able to provide an answer to the question that follows.

Every animal is suitable for a pet if it loves to gaze at the moon.

When I detest an animal, I avoid it.

No animals are carnivorous unless they prowl at night.

No cat fails to kill mice.

No animals ever take to me, except those in this house.

Kangaroos are not suitable for pets.

None but carnivores kill mice.

I detest animals that do not take to me.

The only animals in this house are cats.

Animals that prowl at night always love to gaze at the moon.

Do I avoid kangaroos?

Solution on page 248

In the late 1680, Isaac Newton and Samuel Pepys got into a discussion about rolls of the dice. As president of the Royal Society of London for Improving Natural Knowledge (and a highly effective administrator professionalizing the Royal Navy), Pepys was well aware of Newton's broad expertise in matters mathematical. Indeed, the first edition of Newton's famous *Principia Mathematica* included Pepys' name as imprimatur, effectively endorsing and guaranteeing that the book was of high standard. So, when planning a wager, Pepys naturally turned to Newton for advice. He was considering wagers based on three different dice rolls – rolling six dice to get at least one 6, rolling 12 dice to get at least two 6s, and rolling 18 dice to get at least three 6s. He felt that the largest dice pool would give the most chances for success, and wanted Newton's opinion.

What do you think?

Solution on page 249

SEQUENCES

These sequence puzzles will test your abilities at matching data patterns. There is a very specific reason for the following sequence of letters. Can you figure it out, and find the next one in the list?

D   N   O   S   A   J   ...?

ABCDEFG
HIJKLMN
OPQRSTU
VWXYZ

Solution on page 250

TIME TRAVEL

There is much misunderstanding about relativity. Consider a pair of old-fashioned wind-up pocket watches, identical in every respect. Both are well-wound, functioning normally, and set to exactly the same time. They are both placed in normal rooms, heated to a steady 20°C, and kept well-wound. One room is at sea level, while the other is up a mountain, at an elevation of 4000 feet.

After two weeks, the watches are compared, and the one in the mountain room is found to be noticeably fast compared to its twin. Afterwards, if reset and kept in the same room, it will be seen that both watches once more keep identical time.

Why is this?

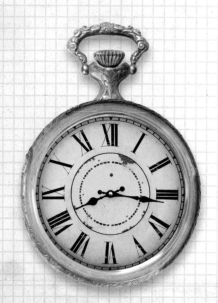

Solution on page 251

CIPHERTEXT

In this puzzle, the challenge is to decrypt a quotation that has been made obscure by the use of a simple cipher. Are you able to work out what it says?

```
AFRSH  LWOMT  EAISE

ETRAI  YHYRN  TETIA

DSAAT  EAEET  ITEDN

TEETR  AIYSA  ATEAS

FAHMT  CRFRO  ELTTE

AEOCR  ANNAF  RSHYR

CRANH  YOORF  ROELT
```

Solution on page 251

GRAVITATIONAL PULL

As we all know, the Moon rotates around the Earth, keeping us company on our trek around the sun. It's unusually large for a satellite (compared to its parent planet), being a quarter of the Earth's diameter, and about one eightieth of its mass – pro rata, none of the other moons in the solar system are larger. Its speed of rotation is locked to the time it takes to orbit the Earth, so it always shows us the same face. This arose because of tidal forces rather than some mystic coincidence, but it is still a lovely factor. However, have you ever wondered why the Moon stays with us? The Sun's gravitational pull on the Moon is more than two times greater than the Earth's pull on it, so why hasn't the Moon gone flying off into the Sun?

Solution on page 252

SEQUENCES

These sequence puzzles will test your abilities at matching data patterns. There is a very specific reason for the following sequence of letters. Can you figure it out, and find the next one in the list?

N   W   H   O   I   I   I   ...?

ABCDEFG HIJKLMN OPQRSTU VWXYZ

Solution on page 253

THE RIDDLE OF THE SPHINX

The most famous riddle of all is probably the Riddle of the Sphinx, from ancient Greek myth. Said to be an Ethiopian monster sent to Thebes by the one of the gods of Olympus, the Sphinx was a treacherous and merciless beast with the body of a lioness, the wings of a monstrous eagle, a snake's tail and a woman's head. It waited at the entrance to the city, demanding an answer to its problem from travellers. When they inevitably failed to solve it, she devoured them. Oedipus was the one who solved the puzzle in the end. Defeated, the Sphinx devoured herself instead. The riddle was: "Which creature has one voice and yet becomes four-footed and two-footed and three-footed?"

Do you know the answer?

Solution on page 253

PILOT PUZZLE

It is said, with some persistence, that during the First World War, a French pilot flying at an altitude of two kilometres noticed an irritating fly by his face. Swatting at it, he was astonished to discover that he'd successfully caught a German bullet. The incident may be apocryphal – the lack of firm information regarding the details seems to suggest as much – but it has been included here because it is, in fact, quite possible. While it seems broadly unlikely, there is nothing about the story which marks it out as fabrication. Can you deduce how such a feat could be possible?

Solution on page 254

BALLOON EXPERIMENT

Imagine that you are in a car at rest on a level road. Perhaps the street outside your home would serve for such a scene. So, within the car, there is a helium-filled balloon whose short string is fixed to the back seat. If you are imagining passengers in the car with you, please ask them to avoid tampering with the balloon for the moment. Your imaginary car, your imaginary rules. The balloon floats freely up from the seat, not being interfered with, and not touching the ceiling. All of the car's windows are closed.

When the car starts and accelerates off, will the balloon move forwards, backwards, or stay in place?

Solution on page 255

> Learn from yesterday, live for today, hope for tomorrow. The important thing is not to stop questioning.

ALBERT EINSTEIN

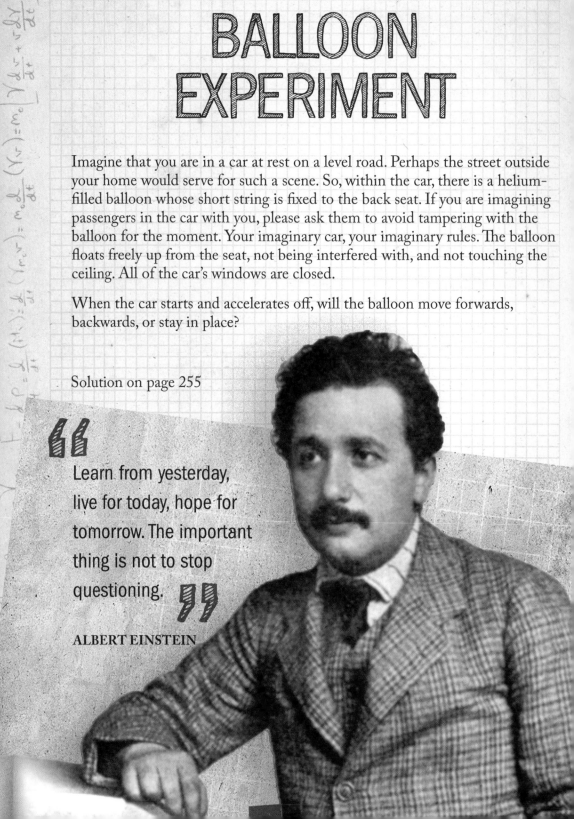

GOOD EGG

Eggs are a marvel of design, a very physical example of evolution's simple elegance. They are also quite tasty, and a vital protein source for millions of people. For our current purposes, however, they are an excellent chance to exercise some scientific curiosity. Imagine that there is an unbroken egg lying on a flat work surface in your kitchen. For some reason, you are reluctant to lift it from the surface. Neither are you prepared to simply break it. Furthermore, the egg is at room temperature, but you have no idea whether it is raw or whether it has been cooked at some previous time. These conditions may seem prohibitive to the point of being contrived, but it is sometimes necessary to take liberties with causality. The question, then, is this: given these restrictions, can you see a simple, tool-free way to tell whether it is raw or cooked?

Solution on page 255

$$R_{\mu\nu} - \frac{1}{2} g_{\mu\nu} R + g_{\mu\nu} \Lambda = \frac{8\pi G}{c^4} T^{\mu\nu} \qquad D = \mu k_B T \qquad T_c = \left(\frac{n}{\zeta(3/2)}\right)^{2/3} \frac{2\pi\hbar^2}{mk_B} \approx 3.3125$$

CHAPTER ONE

PUZZLE ANSWERS

$$\vec{a}_A = \sum_{B \neq A} \frac{G m_B \vec{r}_{BA}}{r^2_{AB}} + \frac{1}{c^2} \sum_{B \neq A} \frac{G m_B \vec{r}_{BA}}{r^2_{AB}} \left[v_A^2 + 2 v_B^2 - 4 (\vec{v}_A \cdot \vec{v}_B) - \frac{3}{2} (\vec{r}_{AB} \cdot \vec{v}_B)^2 \frac{G m_B}{r_{AB}} [\vec{r}_{AB} \cdot (4\vec{v}_A - 3\vec{v}_B)](\vec{v}_A - \vec{v}_B) \right.$$

$$C_v = \left(\frac{\partial U}{\partial T}\right)_v$$

$$R_{\mu\nu} - \frac{1}{2} g_{\mu\nu} R + g_{\mu\nu} \Lambda = \frac{8\pi G}{c^4} T_{\mu\nu}$$

$$\frac{\partial \mathcal{L}_G}{\partial g_{\mu\nu}} - \frac{1}{2} P_{ab} = 0$$

$$\frac{\partial \mathcal{L}_G}{\partial g_{\mu\nu}} + \frac{1}{c^2} \sum_{B \neq A} \frac{G m_B \vec{r}_{BA}}{r^2_{AB}} \left[v_A^2 + 2 v_B^2 - 4(\vec{v}_A \cdot \vec{v}_B) - \frac{3}{2}(\vec{r}_{AB} \cdot \vec{v}_B)^2 \right] \qquad [158] \qquad [\vec{r}_{AB}(4\vec{v}_A - 3\vec{v}_B)](\vec{v}_A - \vec{v}_B) \qquad C_v = \left(\frac{\partial U}{\partial T}\right)_v \quad -\frac{1}{2} P$$

BODIES IN MOTION

You are moving more quickly at night.
Like its orbit around the Sun, the Earth's spin on its axis is anticlockwise. This means that at any given moment, the night side of the planet – being further from the Sun – is moving in the same direction as the orbit, while the day side is moving in the opposite direction. So at midnight, you're moving 30 + 0.5km/s around the Sun, and at midday, you're moving 30 - 0.5km/s.

ABSOLUTELY NOTHING

The error is assuming that the associative law applies to an infinite calculation. That isn't necessarily true. Infinity is uncountable, and therefore indefinite – it goes on for ever, after all – and if your chain of sums isn't fixed, you can't freely rearrange things. It is the chain of infinite (+1-1) and (-1+1) expressions that is equal, not the whole equation.

AN EXERCISE IN LOGIC

No. I only enjoy poems about things which can bear my weight.

ANSWER 4

SUBMERSIBLE

When a submarine is submerged, the water presses in on its shell from all directions at the same time. That means there is as much pressure downwards on the sub as there is upwards, and these balance out, leaving it free to move. If a sub settles onto a rigid ocean floor, however, the water will be displaced from around it, and suddenly all the pressure will be downwards. This can easily be sufficient to lock the sub in place, never to move again.

$$R_{\mu\nu} - \frac{1}{2} g_{\mu\nu} R + g_{\mu\nu} \Lambda = \frac{8\pi G_a}{c^4} T_{\mu\nu}$$

$$\vec{a}_A = \sum_{B \neq A} \qquad T_c = \left(\frac{n}{\zeta(3/2)}\right)^{2/3} \frac{2\pi \hbar^2}{m k_B} \approx 3.3125$$

FORTY-EIGHT

1680.

1,680. 1680+1 = 1681 = 41x41; (1680/2 = 840)+1 = 841 = 29x29.

⟷

MASHED QUOTE

The quotation is:

"When you are courting a nice girl, an hour seems like a second. When you sit on a red-hot cinder, a second seems like an hour. That's relativity."

Albert Einstein

$$\frac{G m_B \vec{n}_{BA}}{r^2{}_{AB}} + \frac{1}{c^2} \sum_{B \neq A} \frac{G m_B \vec{n}_{BA}}{r^2{}_{AB}}$$

$$4 \sum_{c \neq A} \frac{G m_B}{r^2{}_{AB}} [\vec{n}_{AB} (4\vec{v}_A - 3\vec{v}_B)] (\vec{v}_A - \vec{v}_B) - \frac{1}{2} \rho$$

TWO PAILS

They would be the same weight. A floating object displaces
water exactly equal to its weight. Since they are filled to the
same level, they are the same weight, despite the chunk of wood.
Do note, however, that an object which sinks will weigh
more than the liquid it displaces.

HIGH WIRE

A high wire performer remains balanced by keeping his or her centre
of gravity directly above the wire. The bar that is carried helps in two
ways. Most critically, it has its weight concentrated at its ends. These
dip downwards, bringing the athlete's centre of gravity down below the
wire. As a result, the performer is far more stable – and thus safer –
than may seem to be the case. Note that as a secondary benefit,
the bar possesses considerable inertia, and so the athlete can push
against it to make adjustments in balance if required.

CIPHERTEXT

This cipher is a basic one, to get you started. All spaces and punctuations have been removed, and the resulting text broken into blocks of five letters. The last block is rounded up to five characters with junk. Line breaks / indents are irrelevant.

The quotation is:

"A human being is a part of the whole called by us 'universe', a part limited in time and space. He experiences himself, his thoughts and feeling as something separated from the rest, a kind of optical delusion of his consciousness. This delusion is a kind of prison for us, restricting us to our personal desires and to affection for a few persons nearest to us. Our task must be to free ourselves from this prison by widening our circle of compassion to embrace all living creatures and the whole of nature in its beauty."

Albert Einstein

ANSWER 10
FIBONACCI'S GAME

Through the various multiplications, the different elements of the ANSWER – position in line, finger number and joint number – are put into separate digits of the final total. Take away 350, the base value of the set of calculations, and the digits of the result give you seat, finger and joint in that order.

For example, someone in the 8th seat, with a ring on the 2nd joint of finger 4, will result in a total of:

8x2 = 16, +5 = 21, x5 = 105, +10 = 115.

(115 + 4) x 10 = 1190, and

+2 = 1192.

Then, for the performer, 1192-350 = 842, which breaks back down to 8 - 4 - 2.

ANSWER 11
A CURIOUS THOUGHT

Well, it is theoretically possible, but just as certainly unwise. The house would have to be located precisely upon the North Pole. This region consists of constantly shifting sea ice, so construction would be difficult at best, even setting aside the issues of it also being a vastly remote, inhospitable and inaccessible area.

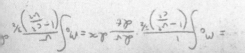

GOLD STANDARD

Solid objects displace not only liquids according to their volume, but also gases. From Archimedes' principle, it can be seen that within the atmosphere of our planet, the reported weight of an object on a scale will be lighter than its true mass would suggest. Specifically, the object will subtract the weight of the air it displaces from its apparent weight. Gold is significantly denser than any wood, and therefore displaces less air, reducing its true weight by less. In a vacuum chamber, the truth would be revealed. The "ton" of wood weighs more than the "ton" of gold.

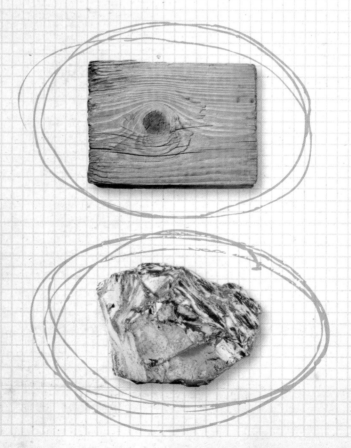

IN A SPIN

There are several good options. For one, drop a spherical object down a tall pipe or shaft (to avoid air currents), and measure how far it deflects from falling straight down. At the equator, a drop of 500 feet will give you an easterly deflection of more than an inch. Another is to weigh yourself precisely at sea-level at the equator, and again at sea-level at one of the poles. You will weigh slightly less at the equator, because you are moving faster there, and the rotational forces help to counteract gravity. You could also drive directly north from the equator to the north pole, and examine the eastwards force acting on your vehicle by carefully measuring pressure on your right-hand tyres. It will be greatest at the equator, and fall to nothing at your destination.

As an aside, it may interest you to know that the sun does actually revolve on its axis, just as the Earth does. It is fluid rather than solid, however, so while its equator revolves once every 27 days, its poles revolve once every 31 days.

SCIENTIFIC LOGIC

New Haven.

Emily, the American scientist in Hanover, studied physics.

Jennifer, the British scientist in Cambridge, studied nanotechnology.

Marianne, the Canadian scientist in New York, studied biochemistry.

Alice, the Australian scientist in Providence, studied metamaterials.

Sophie, the Irish scientist in New Haven, studied astrophysics.

AN EXPERIMENT

Water molecules evaporate off your skin into the air continually. This process is swifter in faster-moving air, because the increased energy encourages more of your sweat to become gaseous. This evaporation cools your skin down. So the slow breath feels more or less the same as its real temperature, while the fast breath seems significantly cooler. In addition, there's a minor factor from gaseous expansion. The gas you force through a small hole spreads out afterwards, and that expansion has a cooling effect – so, in fact, the fast breath does become slightly colder.

A BIT OF POLISH

Ice is not actually a slippery substance. However, its melting point drops when it is pressurized. So when you stand on it – or pull a sledge's runner over it – a small amount melts, and it is the resulting meltwater that is slippery. A rough surface reduces the number of points of contact between the ice and the runner (or foot), increasing the pressure each one is under, and thereby increasing the amount of water produced. In very cold temperatures, where body pressure is insufficient to bring the ice above melt point, ice is no more slippery to walk on than stone is.

TRIBAL MATHEMATICS

Despite the spiritual trappings, this is a sophisticated physical implementation of binary multiplication. The right-hand column, where the value number is halved repeatedly (rounding down), and then even numbers discarded, becomes the binary equivalent of the number in base ten. So here, 22 becomes represented by 10110. Then the left-hand column serves as a way of multiplying the powers of two through for the designated volume number. By starting from the unit value, 7, and then doubling, each column becomes 7x that binary digit. 14 is 7x2, 28 is 7x4, and so on. Because 22 is 10110, 7x22 is (0x1) + (7x2) + (7x4) + (0x8) + (7x16), and adding those stones gives you your final answer. It is just as effective the other way around, of course: 7, halved and rounded, gives 3, which then gives 1. No "evil" evens, so just three holes for 22, 44 and 88 – which, added together, give you 154.

A PROBLEM IN GLASS

Change the window from an orthogonal square to a square diamond – so the five-foot measurement moves from the side-to-side distance to a tip-to-tip diagonal measurement. Then although the window is still 5ft high and wide, the side-to-side distance is just 3.535 feet, and its area is 12.5 sq ft, compared to the original 25 sq ft.

MASHED QUOTE

The quotation is:

"Everybody is a genius. But if you judge a fish by its ability to climb a tree, it will live its whole life believing that it is stupid."

Albert Einstein

$$R_{\mu\nu} - \frac{1}{2} g_{\mu\nu} R + g_{\mu\nu} \Lambda = \frac{8\pi G}{c^4} T_{\mu\nu}$$

$$\vec{a}A = \sum_{B \neq A} \qquad T_c = \left(\frac{n}{\zeta(3/2)}\right)^{2/3} \frac{2\pi \hbar^2}{m k_B} \approx 3.3125$$

CIPHERTEXT

The encryption cipher works by simple substitution, moving each letter of the alphabet one space forward, so that A becomes B, B becomes C, and so on. Word breaks are left alone. Decryption is simply the reversal of this process.

The quotation is:

"If you want your children to be intelligent, read them fairy tales. If you want them to be more intelligent, read them more fairy tales."

Albert Einstein

INFINITE WORLDS

It turns out that the idea of "larger" has to be discarded when considering infinity. Obviously there are twice as many natural numbers as there are even natural numbers for any range. Equally obviously, both sets are infinite, and therefore the same size. The only accurate ANSWER is that the question is meaningless.

SUNLIGHT

6 a.m. Dawn happens when our position on the Earth
rotates into sunlight which has already reached the planet,
so its travel time here is irrelevant.

COFFEE CONUNDRUM

The espresso drinker is Bruce.

Joan is drinking cappuccino, wearing blue, and likes pop.

Bruce is drinking espresso, wearing red, and likes rock.

Steve is drinking cocoa, wearing cream, and likes classical.

Diana is drinking latte, wearing black, and likes electronica.

Megan is drinking tea, wearing green, and likes country.

CHAPTER TWO

PUZZLE ANSWERS

$$R_{\mu\nu} - \frac{1}{2} g_{\mu\nu} R + g_{\mu\nu} \Lambda = \frac{8\pi G_s}{c^4} T_{\mu\nu}$$

$$D = \mu k_B T$$

$$T_c = \left(\frac{n}{\zeta(3/2)}\right)^{2/3} \frac{2\pi \hbar^2}{m k_B} \approx 3.3125$$

$$\vec{a}_A = \sum_{B \neq A} \frac{G_{m_B} \vec{r}_{BA}}{r^2_{AB}} + \frac{1}{c^2} \sum_{B \neq A} \frac{G_{m_B} \vec{r}_{BA}}{r^2_{AB}} \left[v_A^2 + 2v_B^2 - 4(\vec{v}_A \cdot \vec{v}_B) - \frac{3}{2}(\hat{r}_{AB} \cdot \vec{v}_B)^2 \right] \frac{G_{m_B}}{r_{AB}} [\hat{r}_{AB} \cdot (4\vec{v}_A - 3\vec{v}_B)](\vec{v}_A - \vec{v}_B)$$

$$C_V = \left(\frac{\partial U}{\partial T}\right)_V$$

$$C_V = \left(\frac{\partial U}{\partial T}\right)_V$$

$$R_{\mu\nu} - \frac{1}{2} g_{\mu\nu} R + g_{\mu\nu} \Lambda = \frac{8\pi G_s}{c^4} T_{\mu\nu}$$

$$\frac{\delta \int g}{\delta T} + \frac{1}{c^2} \sum_{B \neq A} \frac{G_{m_B} \vec{r}_{BA}}{r^2_{AB}} \left[v_A^2 + 2v_B^2 - 4(\vec{v}_A \cdot \vec{v}_B) - \frac{3}{2}(\hat{r}_{AB} \cdot \vec{v}_B)^2 \right]$$

$$[177]$$

$$[\hat{r}_{AB} \cdot (4\vec{v}_A - 3\vec{v}_B)](\vec{v}_A - \vec{v}_B)$$

$$-\frac{1}{2} P$$

MIRROR, MIRROR

No. Despite everything that common sense suggests, a mirrored surface is effectively invisible. All you can see is the light that it reflects. Much of stage magic relies on the fact that a clean, rimless mirror is invisible.

THE EIGHT QUEENS

There are 12 different possible solutions to this problem. The one most commonly reached (because its underlying principles are known in mathematical circles) is to place the queens at 2a, 4b, 6c, 8d, 3e, 1f, 7g and 5h. Regardless, well done if you managed it.

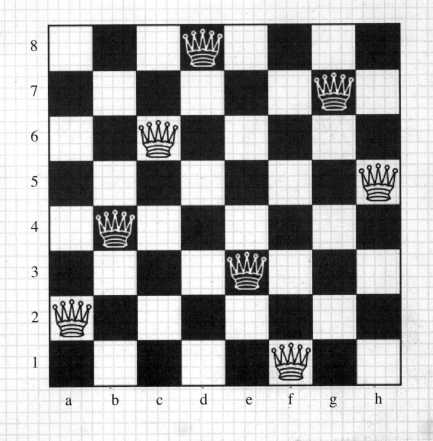

ABSOLUTELY TRUE

No. The only animal that is easy to stroke is the buffalo,
as it does not kick.

ELEVATING

When the elevator is flush with the shaft walls, the air beneath
it provides some cushioning. If the cab were to fall, the
increasingly compressed air would offer increasing resistance,
working against gravity.

A QUESTION OF DISPLACEMENT

The water level will fall. The lead is heavier than the water,
which is why it sinks. When floating – thanks to the boat – it
displaces water equal to its weight, but when submerged, it displaces
water equal to its volume. Since it is heavier than water, its
volume in water is less than its weight in water.

IMITATION OF REALITY

Film producers are quite right that the scream would get fainter as it gets more distant. But it would also reduce in pitch as the screamer accelerates, thanks to the Doppler effect – also why emergency vehicle sirens sound different as they approach you, pass, and then speed away.

TRIAL BY LOGIC

Protective gear.

TekTrex, a Belgian company, sell robotics and are sending
a rep to Glasgow.

Karma, an Italian company, sell designer equipment and are sending
a rep to Barcelona.

3ird Eye, a Portugese company, sell film cameras and are sending
a rep to Frankfurt.

Power Projects, a Danish company, sell protective gear and are sending
a rep to Prague.

C. A. F., a Dutch company, sell leatherwear and are sending
a rep to Paris.

SITTING COMFORTABLY

The issue is one of balance. If you sit straight, as described,
your centre of gravity is located behind your feet (the point where
you are trying to balance). Until you reposition your centre of gravity
over your feet by leaning forward and/or moving your feet back,
you will never be able to stand.

BAREFOOT DOCTOR

The disparity is down to thermal conductivity. Tile conducts heat very effectively, so when you step on it, the heat is quickly drawn from the sole of your foot, and you are aware of the rapid shift in temperature. Carpet, on the other hand, conducts heat very poorly, so your feet lose far less heat. You feel this difference as the carpet being warm while the tile is cold, but the truth is that they are the same temperature in and of themselves.

CIPHERTEXT

The cipher works by simply reversing the entire block of text, so it starts with the last letter and reads back to the first, completely ignoring line-breaks. The quotation is:

"It would be possible to describe everything scientifically, but it would make no sense – it would be without meaning, as if you described a Beethoven symphony as a variation of wave pressure."

Albert Einstein

BALL DROP

9ft. Just before impact, the balls are travelling at an unknown speed of x metres per second. Since the balls are perfectly elastic and the floor perfectly rigid, the heavy ball will hit, and its speed go from x (downward) to $-x$ (upward). In that instant, the light ball will suddenly be travelling at a speed of $2x$ compared to the heavy ball, since x is two more than $-x$. It reflects from the heavy ball, travelling at $-2x$ compared to it – and since the heavy ball is moving at $-x$ already, the light ball is then moving at $-3x$ compared to the floor. Since its energy is dependent on its speed squared, however much energy it gained in falling, it now possesses nine times that energy to rise with.

So it will climb to 9x1ft, or 9ft.

PENDULUM

It would make no difference. Pendulums work entirely by gravity. Since gravity acts on all molecules in an object simultaneously, the weight of the bob is irrelevant. In fact, in a vacuum, the size of the pendulum's bob is likewise of no significance. It is solely dependent on the length of the string.

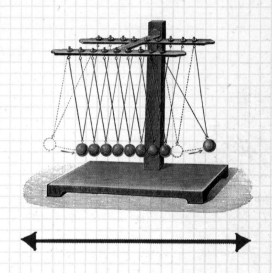

ANSWER 36

TRUE IN ALL PARTICULARS

No. Alcoholics are too untidy to go to parties.

FERMI'S PARADOX

There are seven major classes of assumption that would need to be true for Fermi's question to be a genuine paradox.

1. We will recognize aliens and their activity when we see it/them (i.e., they'd be obvious if they were here/out there). 2. Access to the Earth and surrounding space is unrestricted (i.e., we are not a "nature reserve" or "no-man's land"). 3. If any proof of alien activity was detected, the public would be told (i.e., they're not already here). 4. That the Solar System and its surrounds are interesting enough to attract alien attention/colonization efforts in the first place (i.e., we would have been noticed). 5. That interested aliens could (and would) come here, even if they wanted to (i.e., they'd somehow have faster-than-light travel). 6. That we've been looking when they've been active (i.e., they haven't been here in the past, and won't be in the future). 7. That any alien civilization is actually going to want to expand, explore, and otherwise busy themselves out there (i.e., they wouldn't just stay at home).

Most other objections fall into one of those categories. For example, the idea that maybe they just don't have instruments good enough to spot us out here falls under (4), while the idea that maybe their probes are tiny nanomachines in orbit would fall under (1).

OVERFLOW

In fact, you will be able to add several hundred pins to even a fairly modest full wineglass without spilling any water. After a lot of pins, the water's surface will bulge noticeably, however. The effect happens because of the water's surface tension. The molecules on top of the water act as a sort of net, holding together to prevent spillage. You'll be able to continue until the pressure of the extra volume is greater than the strength of the surface tension – which, as any number of water-skating bugs can tell you, is surprisingly high.

GRAVITY

It's easy. Just find a pair of objects that present the same shape to the air, but have different weights, and drop them. If you have two small, identical boxes – matchboxes say, or lightbulb boxes – you can have one empty, and the other filled with coins. If you didn't mind the mess, you could use a hard-boiled egg, and one that had been blown empty. A ping-pong ball could be filled with sand or water via a small hole. Either way, hold the objects at the same height, at the same orientation, and they'll hit the floor together – at least, they will so long as the lighter one isn't so light as to be delayed by air pressure, as with a feather.

ANSWER 40
COSTLY LOGIC

Lucille's meal was the most expensive.

Burt had a twice-roasted pork belly with ratatouille Provencal, and paid £24.00

Calvin had a rump of lamb with fricassee of spinach, and paid £24.50

Antonia had a venison loin with creamed leeks, and paid £25.50

Neal had a duck breast with wild mushroom risotto, and paid £25.00

Lucille has a fillet of beef with glazed carrots, and paid £26.00

ANSWER 41
MARBLES

You can fit six spheres around the perimeter of a sphere of equal size, if all are in contact with the central one.

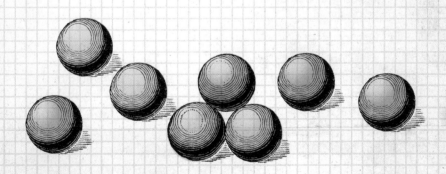

GOING DOWN

Just three metres below ground, the seasonal temperature lag is typically between three and four months. As far as the burrowing creatures are concerned, it would be spring. If you go down further, below 25 metres, the temperature hardly ever changes at all.

ANSWER 43

EXERCISE FOR THE MIND

Yes, because they do not hang their hats on the tap.

CROCODILE CONUNDRUM

If she says the crocodile will return the baby, it is free to eat him. If she says it will eat the baby and it does, then it has to give the baby back – but if it does so before eating him, the mother's prediction is falsified. Since the situation is irreconcilable either way, the crocodile may decide some middle course, such as returning just a leg. It is generally accepted that the best ANSWER is to reply, "I predict that if I correctly predict the fate of my baby, then you will return him. Otherwise, you will eat him." This unarguably cancels all the crocodile's options – so long as it is accepted as a valid prediction.

HOT METAL

The metal keeps the same proportions as it expands, which means that the hole also gets bigger. This is why you can open a tough jar lid by running it under hot water first.

A JOURNEY BY TRAIN

Any particular ratio of speeds between the two trains will result in the pair meeting at a particular point along the track, and thus in particular remaining journey times. You do not need to know how long the track is. If they meet with the same journey time left, for example, they are both travelling at the same speed, and meeting in the middle. If one has two hours left and the other thirty-five, it is impossible for their meeting point to be at three-quarter mark. In this instance, train 1 is twice as fast as train 2, and has covered two-thirds of the distance in the same time that the slower has covered just a third.

CIPHERTEXT

The cipher works by removing punctuation and then rotating each letter 13 places forward in the alphabet (known in computer circles as "ROT-13") – so A becomes N, B becomes O, and so on. The quotation is:

"Heroism at command, senseless brutality, deplorable love-of-country and all the loathsome nonsense that goes by the name of patriotism, how violently I hate all this, how despicable and ignoble war is; I would rather be torn to shreds than be part of so base an action! It is my conviction that killing under the cloak of war is nothing but an act of murder."

Albert Einstein

POWER

It is the exercise of the calf-muscles, either by standing on your toes,
or, while seated, raising the knees while keeping the toes on the floor.
You could lift someone sitting on your knees whom you could
never hope to budge with your arms.

CHAPTER THREE

PUZZLE ANSWERS

$$R_{\mu\nu} - \frac{1}{2} g_{\mu\nu} R + g_{\mu\nu} \Lambda = \frac{8\pi G}{c^4} T_{\mu\nu} \qquad D = \mu k_B T \qquad T_c = \left(\frac{n}{\zeta(3/2)}\right)^{2/3} \frac{2\pi\hbar^2}{mk_B} \approx 3.3125$$

$$\vec{a}_A = \sum_{B \neq A} \frac{G m_B \vec{r}_{BA}}{r^3 AB} + \frac{1}{c^2} \sum_{B \neq A} \frac{G m_B \vec{r}_{BA}}{r^2 AB} \left[\vec{v}_A^2 + 2v^2_B - 4(\vec{v}_A \cdot \vec{v}_B) - \frac{3}{2}(\vec{r}_{AB} \cdot \vec{v}_B)^2 \frac{G m_B}{r AB} [\vec{r}_{AB} \cdot (4\vec{v}_A - 3\vec{v}_B)](\vec{v}_A - \vec{v}_B) \right] \qquad C_V = \left(\frac{\partial U}{\partial T}\right)_V$$

$$C_V = \left(\frac{\partial U}{\partial T}\right)_V \qquad R_{\mu\nu} - \frac{1}{2} g_{\mu\nu} R + g_{\mu\nu} \Lambda = -\frac{8\pi G}{c^4} T_{\mu\nu} \qquad R_{\mu\nu} - \frac{1}{2} g_{\mu\nu} R + \frac{8\pi G}{c^4} P_{ab} = 0 \qquad \frac{\delta L_G}{\delta g^{ab}} + \frac{1}{c^2} \sum_{B \neq A} \frac{G m_B \vec{r}_{BA}}{r^2 AB}$$

$$\left[v_A^2 + 2v^2_B - 4(\vec{v}_A \cdot \vec{v}_B) - \frac{3}{2}(\vec{r}_{AB} \cdot \vec{v}_B)^2 \right] \qquad [194] \qquad [\vec{r}_{AB} \cdot (4\vec{v}_A - 3\vec{v}_B)](\vec{v}_A - \vec{v}_B) \qquad -\frac{1}{2} P$$

MAGIC SQUARE

Incredibly, there are thirteen different ways to divide the square into sets of four numbers, each summing to 34. These are:

1. Rows

2. Columns

3. Diagonals (top left to bottom right, and top right to bottom left)

4. Taking the central four cells (and the groups of four numbers remaining above and below, left and right, and diagonally)

5. Dividing the square into quarters

6. Taking the top or bottom half of each such quarter with the same section of the quarter below it

7. Taking the left or right half of each quarter with the same section of the quarter next to it

8. Taking the top half of each quarter with the bottom half of the quarter diametrically opposed to it

9. Taking the left half of each quarter with the right half of the quarter diametrically opposed to it

10. Taking the same cell from each of the four quarters

11. Taking the same cell from the top two quarters with its diametrically opposed cell in the bottom two quarters

12. Taking the same cell from the leftmost two quarters with its diametrically opposed cell in the rightmost two quarters

13. Taking cells clockwise or anti-clockwise from the quarters in turn as you progress clockwise around them (but to make it trickier, the groups starting top left and bottom right in the top left quarter rotate anticlockwise as you progress, but the other two rotate clockwise)

ANSWER 50
SILVER SPOON

The glass is quick to expand when heated, but slower to transmit heat through its thickness. So the inside of the glass gets hot and expands, but the outside edge remains cool, and stays at the same size. This stretches the glass, which is rigid enough that it snaps. Thicker glassware makes the problem worse rather than better; a thinner glass is quicker to heat all the way through, evening out the internal pressure more swiftly.

ANSWER 51
ART AND LOGIC

Rosing.

Adam went to a gallery in New York, looking for Pre-Raphaelite art, only to be impressed by a work by Barker.

James went to a gallery in Toronto, looking for Cityscapes, only to be impressed by a work by Rosing.

Kara went to a gallery in Frankfurt, looking for Cubism, only to be impressed by a work by Riley.

Pippa went to a gallery in Oxford, looking for Neoclassical, only to be impressed by a work by Newman.

Sebastian went to a gallery in Madrid, looking for Op art, only to be impressed by a work by Haring.

BATHTIME

Not directly, no. Our feet are somewhat larger after immersion in hot water, but not because the heat has made it expand in the way it might a piece of metal. The warmth opens up small capillaries in the skin, increasing bloodflow to the skin, making the skin swell a little. In addition to that, a certain amount of water soaks into the skin, swelling it further, and also making it more tender.

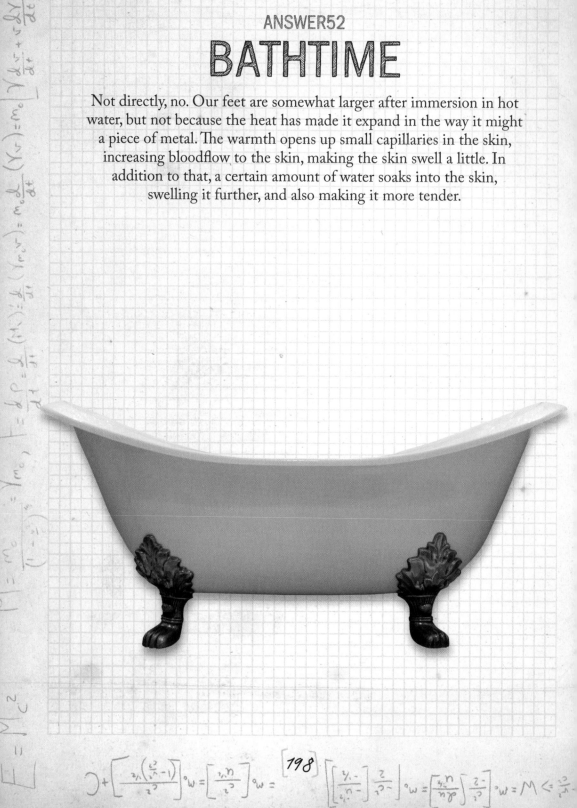

ANSWER 53

BIRTHDAY
PARADOX

Since you can have a valid pairing between any two members of the group, the chances of finding a match increase very rapidly as the group size increases. Just 57 people will give you a 99% chance that two share the same birthday, and you hit a 50% chance at 23 people.

ANSWER 54

ABSOLUTELY TRUE

No, because their dampness makes them ugly.

TWILIGHT

The truth is, of course, that they cannot. Despite appearances, crepuscular rays are still parallel. The divergence is just an optical illusion of perspective, the same way that long, straight roads and train-tracks appear to come together in the distance. It can be difficult to believe, due to the large distances involved and the lack of other objects to make them clear to the eye, but they're just as far apart where they emerge from the cloud (or mountain top).

ON THE BOIL

Water does not boil evenly, moving suddenly from liquid to gas. It heats unevenly, depending on microcurrents in the liquid, dispersal of heat, and assorted other factors. So some of the water molecules reach 100°C and become gas while others are still liquid. These molecules take up more space, pushing the water aside, being lighter, and rise. If they encounter a cold patch of water, they will cool down, and collapse back into water, imploding. These implosions are the source of the sound you hear as the water boils. As the water gets close to boiling point, the chance of a bubble of gas cooling decreases – and so the volume does too.

ANSWER 57

WOOLLY PROBLEM

A scarf.

Radka is using blue wool to make a sweater for a friend.

Kristen is using mauve wool to make a blanket for a spouse.

Hope is using indigo wool to make a scarf for a neighbour.

Ebony is using red wool to make socks for a niece.

Delmer is using grey wool to make a hat for a lover.

THE ILLUSIONIST

As with many conjurer's tricks, the answer lies with mirrors, of course.
A mirror placed between the table legs can be set to seemingly reflect
just the empty floor you'd expect to see. Behind it, the assistant
crouches. When the box goes onto the table, the assistant
unhinges a flap in the table, and pushes his head up through the gap.

TAN LINES

Sand is a significantly more effective reflector of sunlight than other typical surfaces, including grass, stone, water and earth. Spending time at the beach simply exposes you to more sun. Snow is another excellent reflector, but the temperatures it requires means that it is difficult to expose much skin to its tanning effects. As an aside, please do note that tanning damages your skin, ageing you and increasing your risks of skin cancer.

CIPHERTEXT

The Atbash cipher works by switching letters of the alphabet with the letters that would be in their position if the alphabet was reversed, so in other words A becomes Z, B becomes Y, and so on. It was originally designed for Hebrew messages. The quotation is:

"The most beautiful thing we can experience is the mysterious. It is the source of all true art and all science. He to whom this emotion is a stranger, who can no longer pause to wonder and stand rapt in awe, is as good as dead: his eyes are closed."

Albert Einstein

THE PRISONER'S DILEMMA

Dresher and Flood's dilemma has a lot of interesting ramifications, and there are literally entire volumes of academic study devoted to it. To the individual, the best option is to speak up. If B is silent, A gains freedom rather than six months in prison; if B speaks up, A gets five years rather than ten. However, if both prisoners speak up, this strategy leads to an automatic third-worst outcome – hence the dilemma. The "best" strategy is a losing strategy.

ANSWER 62
LAMPLIGHT

The mesh allows gases in, but prevents the flames from escaping. The holes are too small. The grid breaks the flame into tiny pieces, and then the metal absorbs some of the heat, so that the individual mote of flame goes out. It's extremely important not to let the mesh get damaged, though; even one broken link may prove enough to allow a flamelet to survive, with catastrophic consequence.

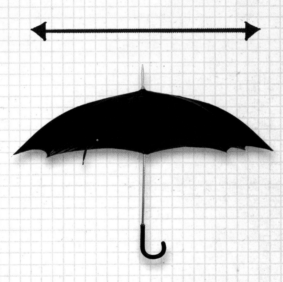

ANSWER 63
STATEMENT OF FACT

Yes. It never rains other than on a Wednesday, and all Wednesdays are cloudy.

SEQUENCE

The next letter is S. The sequence is the first letters of the even numbers in ascending order: Two, Four, Six, Eight, Ten, Twelve, Fourteen and Sixteen.

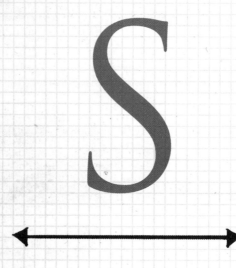

SUNLIGHT

The pieces of cloth will sink into the snow by differing amounts depending on their relative darkness and brightness. This is caused by the cloth warming up in the sun, and melting the snow beneath it. Most likely, the white piece will not have sunk at all, while the black piece may have sunk far enough to be entirely shaded. The coloured pieces will be somewhere in between, according to their specific brightnesses – yellow almost certainly the least, blue or indigo probably the deepest.

$$\frac{d\gamma}{d\beta} = \frac{d}{d\beta}\left(\frac{1}{(1-\beta^2)^{1/2}}\right) = -\frac{1}{2}(-2\beta)(1-\beta^2)^{-3/2} = \beta(1-\beta^2)^{-3/2} \quad \therefore F = m_0\left[\gamma\frac{ds}{dt} \cdots\right]$$

207

BICYCLE REVOLUTIONS

The front wheel, being the one used for steering,
follows a more wobbly course than the rear.
Therefore it travels a greater distance.

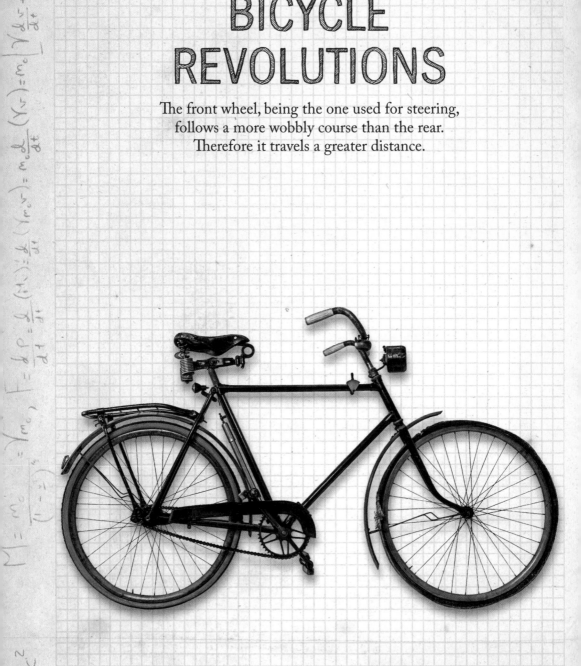

PRESENT LOGIC

Three years.

Randolph has been married to Eunice for seven years,
and has bought her lingerie.

Len has been married to Irma for 16 years,
and has bought her bracelet.

Michael has been married to Anita for three years,
and has bought her a fur coat.

Terrell has been married to Mercedes for 14 years,
and has bought her a book.

Jeffrey has been married to Elisha for five years,
and has bought her a necklace.

THE SANDS OF TIME

For the vast majority of the sand's falling, the answer is no.
The weight missing from the falling sand is balanced by the
extra pressure from sand hitting the bottom. However, there
is a very short reduction in weight when the glass is first turned
over, before any sand reaches the floor. This is balanced
out by a similarly short increase of weight when there is
no more sand starting to fall, but it has not all landed.

THE COIN CHALLENGE

Obtain a fair-sized glass, a piece of paper, and a lighter or match.
Light the paper, and while it is still burning, drop it into the glass.
Then swiftly put the glass down, base up, on the plate. The
paper will go out, and then shortly afterwards, the water will
be sucked into the glass as the cooling air shrinks in volume.
The coin will not move. After a minute or two of drying time,
the coin will be ready to be picked up.

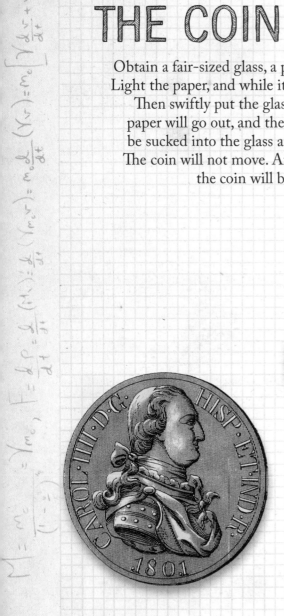

IS THAT A FACT?

Yes. Heavy fish are contemptible, which means that they are
not well turned out.

ANSWER 71

RAVENS

The problem is in assuming that "proof" means "total proof"
rather than "some supporting proof". The logic is correct; the
existence of a green apple does absolutely rule out one non-black
thing from being a raven, increasing the likelihood of all ravens
being black. It just doesn't increase the likelihood by very *much*.

ANSWER 72
SHOOTING STARS

More meteors can be seen after midnight than before because the earth, as it moves in its orbit, sweeps up meteoroids before it. After midnight an observer is on the side of the earth that faces the direction of the earth's orbital motion; before midnight an observer is effectively in earth's meteoritic shadow.

ANSWER 73
SIMPLICITY

A third. If you have three fourths, then a fourth is one third of that amount, not a quarter.

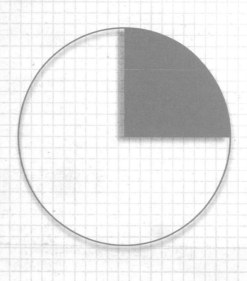

CIPHERTEXT

The cipher works on the basis of simple substitution, but each single letter of the original is replaced with the same 2-letter pair. The first letter of each pair is three places along from the original letter. The second letter is just a distraction. So A always becomes DR, B becomes ET, C becomes FY, and so on.

The quotation is: "Energy cannot be created or destroyed, it can only be changed from one form to another."

Albert Einstein

THAT'S NO MOON...

The object would remain where it was, floating. Newton's shell theorem proved that a symmetrical sphere exerts no net gravitational force on an object inside itself (although it would attract an object outside). As you get closer to one spot on the shell, its gravitational pull gets stronger, but there is a corresponding increasing in the number of spots pulling you in other directions. It evens out to zero. But note that there is no actual place with perfectly zero gravity, so even if the asteroid were well outside the Solar System, the Milky Way itself would still exert a gravitational pull. You wouldn't be able to observe it from inside, but the asteroid and its contents would effectively be in the same free-fall pattern.

ANSWER 76
THE FLY

The trains are both travelling at 50km/h, so they will close a distance of 100km in 1 hour. The fly is moving constantly at 75km/h, so in an hour, it will travel 75km.

ANSWER 77
UP IN SMOKE

It's clearly the same smoke, but the lit end creates an upwards current of warm air, which helps lift the smoke. The smoke is also lighter, because it is warm. At the other end, there is no up-draft (instead, there's a retardant in-draft), and the smoke has cooled as it travels through the cigarette. As the smoke particles are heavier than air and lack any upward compulsion, they sink.

THINK LOGICALLY

Andover.

Delmer is taking rice to Birmingham in a green truck.

Isaac is taking apples to Manchester in a red truck.

James is taking beef to Andover in a white truck.

Krista is taking milk cartons to York in a blue truck.

Omar is taking flour to Cambridge in a grey truck.

CHAPTER FOUR

PUZZLE ANSWERS

$$R_{\mu\nu} - \tfrac{1}{2} g_{\mu\nu} R + g_{\mu\nu} \Lambda = \frac{8\pi G_A}{c^4} T_{\mu\nu}$$

$$D = \mu k_B T$$

$$T_c = \left(\frac{n}{\zeta(3/2)}\right)^{2/3} \frac{2\pi \hbar^2}{m k_B} \approx 3.3125$$

$$\vec{a}_A = \sum_{B \neq A}$$

$$C_V = \left(\frac{\partial U}{\partial T}\right)_V$$

$$\frac{G_m B^{\tilde{n} B_A}}{r^2 AB} + \frac{1}{c^2} \sum_{B \neq A} \frac{G_m B^{\tilde{n} B_A}}{r^2 AB} \left[V_A^2 + 2 V_B^2 - 4(\vec{V}_A \cdot \vec{V}_B) - \tfrac{3}{2}(\vec{n}_{AB} \cdot \vec{V}_B)^2 \right]$$

$$R_{\mu\nu} - \tfrac{1}{c^2} g_{\mu\nu} R + g_{\mu\nu} \Lambda = \frac{8\pi G_A}{c^4} T_{\mu\nu}$$

$$R_{\mu\nu} - \tfrac{1}{2} P_{ab} = 0 \qquad \frac{\delta G}{g^{ab}} - \tfrac{1}{2} P_{ab} = 0$$

$$\sum_{B \neq A} \frac{r^2 AB}{G_m B^{\tilde{n} B_A}} - \frac{G_m B^{\tilde{n} B_A}}{r^2 AB}$$

$$\left[V_A^2 + 2 V_B^2 - 4(\vec{V}_A \cdot \vec{V}_B) - \tfrac{3}{2}(\vec{n}_{AB} \cdot \vec{V}_B)^2 \right]$$

$$[\vec{n}_{AB} (4 \vec{V}_A - 3 \vec{V}_B)] (\vec{V}_A - \vec{V}_B) \qquad -\tfrac{1}{2} P$$

ANSWER 79
COOLING OFF

Hot air rises, but cool air sinks. So the best ANSWER is not to
put the box on top of the ice, but to put the box beneath it. That
way you still get the benefits of direct contact, and you also get cold
air continuously flowing down the sides of the box.

ANSWER 80
NEEDLEPOINT

Reducing out the specific mathematics, since the landing angle of
the needle varies, the point of the needle effectively becomes a point
on a circle. Imagine a coin landing between the seams. This brings
pi into the mix, from where it can then be worked out once you
know the probability.

ANSWER 81
THE SWEET TRUTH

No. True happiness and common sense are mutually exclusive.

RISING UP

Tossing the brick into the dinghy will displace water equal to the brick's weight. Tossing it into the water will displace water equal to its volume. Since the brick is heavier than water, its weight displaces more water than its volume. So toss the brick into the boat for maximum effect. (Yes, global shipping does have an effect on sea-level: it raises it by something like six-millionths of a metre – which, sadly, is more than the combined sea life of the world does).

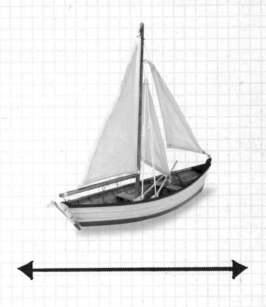

ANSWER 83

BARREL

The trick is to tip the barrel gently on its side until the water touches the lip, and then look inside. If any of the bottom of barrel is visible, it's more than half empty; if any of the barrel wall is obscured, it is more than half full. If it is precisely half-full, the water level will be at the join.

ANSWER 84
RISING CHIMP

Because the rope can move freely, the two loads will automatically balance their positions. Whatever the chimp does, the weight will match – effectively, to gain a foot in height, the chimp has to climb two feet of rope. They will reach the top at the same time.

ANSWER 85

LOGIC PUZZLE

Central Park.

Robin went to SoHo for a board meeting and paid $60.

Annie went to Central Park to see a client and paid $65.

Marcella went to 54th and Lexington to survey property, and paid $70.

Kathleen went to Grand Central Station talent-scouting and paid $75.

Virginia went to Liberty Island on a photographic assignment and paid $80.

DRAUGHTS

On a cold day, the windows and exterior walls will cool down. The air in your room near the window gets colder, which makes it heavier. It sinks, pulling warmer air into the space it vacates. That too chills, and sinks. The result is a circular draft, running along the ceiling from your heat sources to your windows, and along the floor out from the windows and back to the heat sources. This manifests as a cold draft from the window, particularly on your feet and ankles.

SALT

Rice is much more water-absorbent than salt is.
As moisture gets into the cellar, the rice quickly soaks
it up, leaving the flow of salt unimpeded.

ANSWER 88

CIPHERTEXT

The cipher works by misdirection. Only the first letter of each
five-letter block means anything. These first letters spell out the
quotation in the correct order. The quotation is:

"You have to learn the rules of the game. And then you
have to play better than anyone else."

Albert Einstein

ZENO'S RACECOURSE

The Dichotomy assumes that space can be divided infinitely, but time cannot. Both of these assumptions are arbitrary, and at least one of them is wrong. In fact, modern physics suggests a minimum sub-division of space, at the subatomic level.

ZHNΩN

EGG IN A BOTTLE

You need to soak the egg in vinegar for half a day or so. This will make the shell turn quite malleable. Then drop lighted paper into the bottle, and place the egg over the neck. When the air cools and contracts after the flames go out, the egg will be drawn inside. All that then remains is to rinse the inside of the bottle thoroughly with cold water, to both wash out the ashes, and to restore the shell to normal.

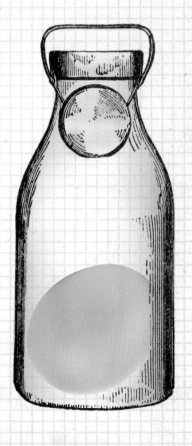

EXERCISE IN LOGIC

Yes. I only own animals I trust.

BERTRAND'S CHOICE

There are three gold coins you could have received, with each having a chance of 1/3, 1/3 and 1/3. In two of those cases, the coin remaining in the box is gold; in just one is it silver. So your chance of a second gold coin is actually 2/3 – rather than the 1/2 that intuition might suggest.

WARM THOUGHTS

The answer, of course, is that the coat does not warm you up directly. Instead, it prevents the perfectly normal loss of your body heat to the surrounding air. In other words, you heat yourself. Wool and fur contain lots of trapped air, and air is an excellent insulating substance. The heat of your body is turned back to you, and thus you get warmer.

ANSWER 94

CHIAROSCURO

This problem can be solved using the geometric relationships of similar triangles and differentiating with respect to time, but is also easily solved graphically with a pencil, ruler and scrap of paper (in the best scientific tradition). When standing immediately under the lamp your shadow will be at your feet, its displacement zero. When you have walked a distance (x) equivalent to your height, it is possible to determine graphically that the tip of your shadow will have moved ($2x$), or twice that distance. Checking for several distances will reassure you that this relationship is constant, although the value of this ratio is dependant upon the relative heights of the person and light source. So, in this simple case we could say that the tip of the shadow is moving at twice the speed of your own pace … but be careful, Einstein would remind us that all things are relative. Only to a stationary observer does the shadow appear to travel at twice your rate. From your point of view, the tip of your shadow is moving away from you at a speed equal to your own pace.

TESTING TRIAL

Felicia and her friend went to the Antarctic.

Lindsey went to an Argentinean lodge with a sibling.

Yolanda went to a Iceland city with a cousin.

Felicia went to an Antarctic outpost with a friend.

Lorrie went to a Japanese villa with a colleague.

Taylor went to a Mauritanian hotel with a parent.

ANSWER 96

GOLF BALLS

In part, the dimples provide an irregular surface to trap air, which reduces the wake of the ball. This reduces drag, increasing distance. More importantly, drivers give backspin to a ball, and the spinning dimples catch air and push it downwards.

The greater air pressure below the ball then imparts lift, and this allows the ball to fly far further than it would.

LEAPING FROM A MOVING BUS

You have two problems to overcome. When you jump, you are moving at the same speed as the bus. The ground, however, is stationary. This provides two problems. You want to minimize your speed before landing, and you want to minimize the chance of falling over. If you jump in the same direction as the bus is moving, you will be facing in the direction of travel – by far the safest way to land – but you will add to your speed. If you jump in the opposite direction, you will minimize your speed, but your body isn't designed to deal with backwards speed, and worse, when you fall over, you won't have your hands in front of you to break your fall. Jumping straight out from the bus leaves you even less balanced when landing, and doesn't reduce your speed at all.

So, if you have to jump, the best option is probably to face the direction of travel, but jump in the opposite direction, backwards. That reduces your speed the most, but you land facing the same direction as your momentum is pushing you. This gives you the best chance of avoiding a catastrophic mishap.

ANIMAL LOGIC

No. I never notice badgers.

ZENO'S STADIUM

Obviously, Zeno is making a ridiculous error. Absolute speed is not relative speed, and the runners pass each other quickly because they're going in opposite directions. But... relativity is an inescapable tyrant. If the runners were in fact spaceships, travelling at nearly the speed of light past each other in opposite directions, they would still pass each other at the speed of light, not nearly twice the speed of light. The truth is that Zeno is accurately describing reality, at least at relativistic speed. The implications that this has for the nature of time are still being debated. We live in a very odd universe.

ANSWER 100

BUBBLES

The bubbles would still attract each other. Water between the two bubbles will be drawn towards the greatest concentration of mass, which is out of the path between the two bubbles. Thus the bubbles will move towards each other.

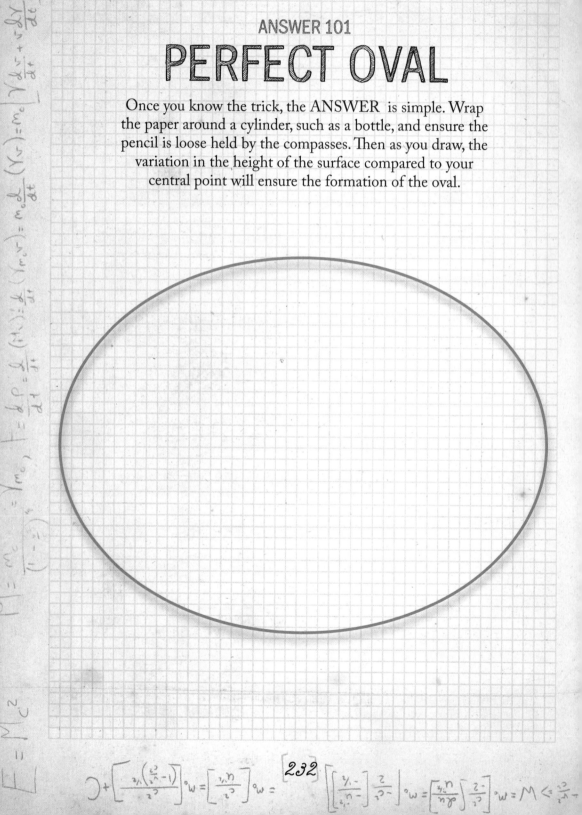

PERFECT OVAL

Once you know the trick, the ANSWER is simple. Wrap the paper around a cylinder, such as a bottle, and ensure the pencil is loose held by the compasses. Then as you draw, the variation in the height of the surface compared to your central point will ensure the formation of the oval.

ANSWER 102
CIPHERTEXT

The cipher works by replacing the letters of the alphabet with the numbers 1-9 in order. Once the alphabet reaches J, it starts from 1 again. So A, J and T are all represented by "1". Spaces are removed in this instance, so the third "9" is unused. The final zeroes are fillers. The quotation is:

"If my theory of relativity is proven successful, Germany will claim me as a German and France will declare me a citizen of the world. Should my theory prove untrue, France will say that I am a German, and Germany will declare that I am a Jew."

Albert Einstein

ANSWER 103
IMPOSSIBLE THINGS

After 52 doublings in height, your card stack would be around 1.23x10^15mm tall – which works out at about 770 million miles, or more than eight times the distance from the Earth to the Sun.

SCHRÖDINGER'S CAT

Quantum mechanics theory suggested that the cat would be in an impossible half-state, both simultaneously alive and dead, until someone opened the chamber to look. In the instant that an observer did check, the cat's fate would be resolved one way or another, and it would either be alive or dead, possibly long dead. To Schrödinger's horror (and Einstein's, too), this turned out to be an absolutely accurate illustration of the way the universe works. Until a process is observed, it is in all possible states simultaneously. The Schrödinger's Cat principle has already been used to create communication streams that show, by their nature, if they have been observed or not.

SCALES

By bending forward, your trunk muscles pull at the lower half of your body, diminishing the pressure on the scales. You can see the opposite effect by pulling yourself as erect as possible, which makes your trunk muscles push down on your lower half, increasing your weight. In addition to this factor, if you bend, you may deflect your centre of gravity away from being directly over the scales, which will also reduce your apparent weight.

THINK LOGICALLY

Robin, in the yellow pyjamas, caught measles, and received a toy.

Alexis had mumps, got ice cream, and wore blue pyjamas.

Billie had tonsilitis, got a visit from a friend, and wore green pyjamas.

Frankie had chicken pox, got jelly, and wore orange pyjamas.

Lee had scarlet fever, got a book, and wore red pyjamas.

Robin had measles, got a toy, and wore yellow pyjamas.

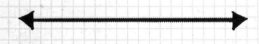

WEIGHTY PROBLEMS

Maximum weight means maximum gravity. If the Earth had even density, maximum gravity would occur as near to the centre as possible while still remaining on its surface – i.e., at the north or south pole. As you move further from the centre, the gravitational pull decreases, so you'd weigh less up a mountain. However, it also decreases when you break the surface, as the mass behind you counterbalances the pull.

In reality, the Earth is not uniformly dense. The core is far heavier, and the balance point where the extra pull from getting closer to the core is outweighed by the pull of the mass above you is 2885km down on average. This seam is called the Gutenberg discontinuity.

ZENO'S ARROW

Things move, and possess momentum. However, if you look at the world from the view of classical physics, where reality is a spatial construct split up into frozen slices of time, then there is indeed no logical point for motion to occur in. Quantum mechanics, having largely replaced classical physics at the very small level, is even worse. It has been conclusively shown that if you know a particle's location, you cannot know its direction or speed (and vice versa). Zeno, knowing where the arrow is hanging in air, is absolutely correct that he cannot say it is moving.

As if that wasn't enough, the Quantum Zeno effect was measured in 1977. This shows that if you observe a quantum system with full attention, its normal passage through time is interrupted. Watching the metaphorical arrow actually makes it stop. Some historic accounts suggest that Zeno was eventually executed, at the age of 60, by being thrown into a massive mortar and pounded to death by an equally massive pestle – for his part in a plot to overthrow a tyrant.

$$R_{\mu\nu} - \tfrac{1}{2}g_{\mu\nu}R + g_{\mu\nu}\Lambda = \frac{8\pi G}{c^4}T_{\mu\nu} \qquad D = \mu k_B T \qquad T_c = \left(\frac{n}{\zeta(3/2)}\right)^{2/3}\frac{2\pi\hbar^2}{mk_B} \approx 3.3125$$

CHAPTER FIVE
PUZZLE ANSWERS

$$C_V = \left(\frac{\partial U}{\partial T}\right)_V$$

$$\vec{a}_A = \sum_{B \neq A} \frac{G m_B \hat{r}_{BA}}{r^2_{AB}} + \frac{1}{c^2}\sum_{B \neq A} \frac{G m_B \hat{r}_{BA}}{r^2_{AB}}\left[v_A^2 + 2v_B^2 - 4(\vec{v}_A \cdot \vec{v}_B) - \tfrac{3}{2}(\vec{r}_{AB}\cdot\vec{v}_B)^2 \frac{G m_B [\vec{r}_{AB}(4\vec{v}_A - 3\vec{v}_B)](\vec{v}_A - \vec{v}_B)}{r_{AB}}\right]$$

$$C_V = \left(\frac{\partial U}{\partial T}\right)_V$$

$$R_{\mu\nu} - \tfrac{1}{2}g_{\mu\nu}R + g_{\mu\nu}\Lambda = \frac{8\pi G}{c^4}T_{\mu\nu} \qquad R_{\mu\nu} - \tfrac{1}{2}g_{\mu\nu} - \tfrac{1}{2}P_{ab} = 0 \qquad \frac{\delta I_G}{\partial T_G} - \tfrac{1}{2}P_{ab} = 0$$

$$\sum_{B \neq A} \frac{r^2_{AB}}{G m_B \hat{r}_{BA} r^2_{AB}} + \frac{1}{c^2}\sum_{B \neq A} \frac{r^2_{AB}}{G m_B \hat{r}_{BA} r^2_{AB}}$$

$$\left[v_A^2 + 2v_B^2 - 4(\vec{v}_A \cdot \vec{v}_B) - \tfrac{3}{2}(\vec{r}_{AB}\cdot\vec{v}_B)^2 \qquad [238] \qquad [\vec{r}_{AB}(4\vec{v}_A - 3\vec{v}_B)](\vec{v}_A - \vec{v}_B) \qquad -\tfrac{1}{2}\rho\right.$$

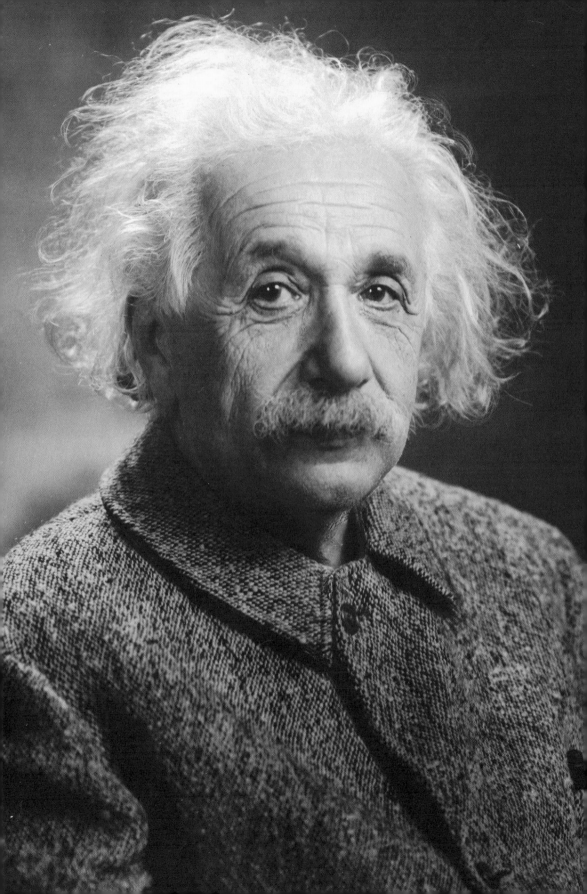

TRUE STATEMENTS

Yes. Your cheques are all marked "not negotiable".

SURVIVAL INSTINCT

In fact, yes. In this situation, you could build up a speed of several miles an hour. When your body moves towards the bow to set up the pull, friction prevents the boat from sliding backwards in reaction. Then, when you pull, the force of the jerk is sufficient to overcome friction, and move the boat forward as your body goes backwards.

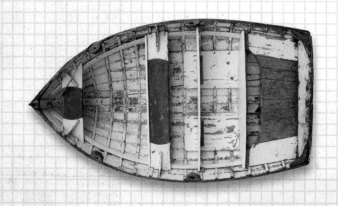

ANSWER 111

THE HUNDRED

The ANSWER is brilliantly simple. 123 - 45 - 67 + 89 = 100.

123456789

←——————————→

ANSWER 112

UNDER PRESSURE

The pressure of the air is balanced out by our blood pressure,
and the concomitant pressure of the liquids inside each of our cells.
This is why certain speculative fiction writers have suggested
that a person in bare vacuum would explode – from the internal
pressures. In truth, we know that this is not the case.

PURE LOGIC

Bertha purchased 15 quail eggs.

Franklyn bought 12 duck eggs and wore a magenta coat.

Byron bought six goose eggs and wore a yellow coat.

Lou bought nine chicken eggs and wore a white coat.

Bertha bought 15 quail eggs and wore a cyan coat.

Megan bought three turkey eggs and wore a black coat.

WATERLINE

When the water boils, the steam pushes water out in a jet.
The comparative coolness of the exhaust pipe collapses the steam
back into water, and new water is sucked up into the boiler, to repeat
the process. The reason it moves is that the expelled water flows in
a straight line, giving all its power forward, while the sucked-in
water comes from 180° around the pipe exit, so that the
backwards pull is largely dispersed. A simple thrust augmenter,
as used in jet engines, could further convert most of this
backwards pull into forwards force by redirecting it.

CIPHERTEXT

This cipher is another misdirection. This time, the quotation is spelled out by just the middle letters of each five-letter block. The quotation is:

"Force always attracts men of low morality."

Albert Einstein

ANSWER 116

THE GRAND HOTEL

Infinity is unlimited. Although there are an infinite amount of existing guests, the manager can ask them to each move from their current room to the room that is twice its number. Then there are infinitely many odd-numbered rooms available for the new arrivals. There are other options too, of course, such as asking everyone to move up one room and booking one new guest in, then repeating that process infinitely.

Hilbert's Hotel is a perfectly accurate description of how infinity works. However, it is so totally counterintuitive that some critics (mainly religious scholars) have cited the paradox as evidence for the non-existence of infinity.

$$\frac{dY}{dt} = \frac{dY}{dv}\frac{dv}{dt} = \frac{dY}{dv}a \quad, \quad \frac{dV}{dv} = \frac{d}{dv}\left(\frac{1}{(1-\frac{v^2}{c^2})^{1/2}}\right) = \frac{dV}{d\beta}\frac{d\beta}{dv}$$

$$E = Mc^2$$

SEQUENCES

The next letter is P. Each time, the letters go up
by three places in the alphabet.

ABCDEFG
HIJKLMN
OPQRSTU
VWXYZ

THINK LOGICALLY

No. They are not written on blue paper.

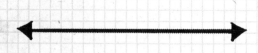

BERRY PARADOX

The resolution lies in the nature of language. "Define" is a vague term, and "the smallest positive integer not definable in 12 words or less" is so imprecise as to be mathematically meaningless.

BALLISTICS

Barely 4km. Air resistance is a far greater impedance than we intuitively feel.

TIME AND TIDE

The moon does indeed pull the sea up towards it, causing a bulge.
But it also pulls the solid body of the Earth towards it as well,
away from the water on the far side. So the high tide on the far
side of the Earth is caused by the planet being pulled away.

TRIAL BY LOGIC

The tea-drinker is Tripp, who is attending an art class.

Nessa is discussing metaphysics, eats choc chip cookies, and drinks soda.

Saldana is acting in a play, eats garibaldi biscuits, and drinks water.

Tripp is attending an art class, eats ginger snaps, and drinks tea.

Tristan is learning French, eats digestives, and drinks coffee.

Vilma is in a reading group, eats butter biscuits, and drinks juice.

ANSWER 123
THE DRIFT

It's all to do with the flow of the wind. A large, flat surface causes the wind to divert much further away from itself than something thin and round, like a pole, or readily air-permeable, like a hedge. The pole gets more snow hitting it because the wind blows it very close.

ANSWER 124
LOGICAL ASSUMPTION

Yes, they do not take to me.

NEWTON-PEPYS

The biggest chance of success is with the smallest pool, 6 dice. As Newton pointed out, you could think of each of the larger pools in terms of multiples of the smaller. With 6 dice, you need to get only one win. With 12, you need to get two wins simultaneously, and with 18, three wins. It's not quite that simple – Pepys was correct in that there are more ways to win with 18 dice than with 6 – but the extra ways don't outbalance the extra difficulty. (For the record, your chances of success are 0.67, 0.62 and 0.60 on the 6-, 12- and 18-die pools respectively.)

SEQUENCES

The next letter is J. The sequence is made up of the first letters of the months in reverse order: December, November, October, September, August, July and June.

JUNE

ABCDEFG
HIJKLMN
OPQRSTU
VWXYZ

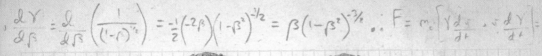

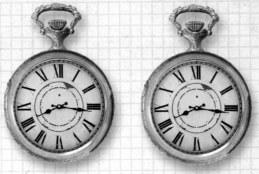

TIME TRAVEL

Relativity has nothing to do with this matter. At high altitudes, air pressure is lower. This means the watch spring has less resistance to overcome, and it is able to move more quickly. The watch thus runs faster.

CIPHERTEXT

The Railfence cipher works by transposition. The text is broken up into two segments, made up by alternating the letters of the original. So the sequence ABCDEFGHIJ would break up into ACEGI BDFHJ. Find the midpoint, and then read alternating letters from the start and the midpoint. The quotation is:

"As far as the laws of mathematics refer to reality, they are not certain; and as far as they are certain, they do not refer to reality."

Albert Einstein

GRAVITATIONAL PULL

The moon is orbiting the sun, just as we are. The Earth has enough pull to keep the moon spinning around us, but that doesn't change the fact that it's still in a solar orbit.

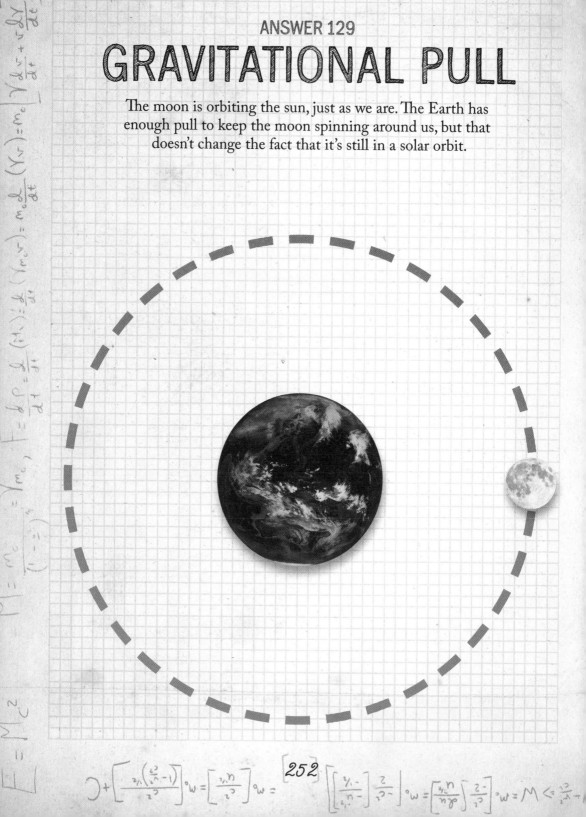

SEQUENCES

The next letter is E. The sequence is made up of the
second letters of the integers in ascending order:
oNe, tWo, tHree, fOur, fIve, sIx, and then sEven.

THE RIDDLE OF THE SPHINX

The solution is a human being, who crawls as a newborn,
walks erect as an adult and uses a walking stick in old age.

PILOT PUZZLE

Bullets may start out very fast, but they do not stay that way. If shot in mid-air, a bullet's horizontal speed will gradually decrease to zero, even as its downward speed increases. An open-cockpit airplane flying at 90mph could easily find itself matched in velocity with a bullet at some point in its flight, so from the pilot's point of view it would seem to be nearly stationary.